Think
like a
PSYCHOLOGIST

D0061769

Think like a PSYCHOLOGIST

Get to grips with the workings of the human mind

Anne Rooney

This edition published in 2019 by Arcturus Publishing Limited
26/27 Bickels Yard, 151–153 Bermondsey Street,
London SE1 3HA

AD006840UK

Printed in the UK

CONTENTS

What is psychology anyway?

The human brain is the single most compelling object of study or contemplation. Whatever interests you may have – art, politics, literature, sport, mechanics, astronomy, chess – they all originated with a human mind and you use your own mind to pursue them. How the mind works, in sickness and in health, is the realm of psychology.

To know how and why and what we think has fascinated humankind for millennia, but until recently we had little other than metaphor and stories to help us express our ideas about our minds' workings.

Brain and mind, body and spirit

In the 17th century, the French philosopher and mathematician René Descartes suggested that the human body works rather like a machine. We can apply fluid dynamics to explain how the blood flows, for instance, and our bones and muscles work just like levers. But Descartes could not work out how the spirit which animates the body – what would later be called 'the ghost in the machine' – fits in.

'I think therefore I am,' he said (in a different philosophical enquiry). We would probably all agree it is principally our

minds that make us who we are. In theory, your physical body could be occupied by another brain (if we had the surgical skill to effect a brain transplant), and that body would no longer act for 'you' but for the person whose brain was residing in it. We locate the 'I' that is our identity in our mind, which is somehow in, or created by our brain.

René Descartes

To explain the mind in the brain, people have turned to stories and religions. Is it a spirit or soul breathed into us by God? Is it a portion of some vast world or universal soul, a little chip off a cosmic block of consciousness? Today, we are getting closer to understanding how the brain works and although we still can't quite locate or define the mind, we can explain a lot of how it works in terms of neurology.

Psychology, psychiatry and neurology

Psychology is the study of how the mind (psyche) works. Psychiatry applies some of that knowledge therapeutically to help people with disorders of the mind. And neurology is the study of the physical and chemical structure and functioning of the brain. In studying 'how the mind works', psychology involves neurology in some of its explanations.

Mind how you go

Many of us might be affected by certain types of mental illness from time to time, just as our bodies may be affected by various physical ailments. You might sometimes have anxiety problems, or suffer a period of depression, or have obsessive-compulsive disorder (OCD), just as you may have had appendicitis or have suffered from eczema or asthma.

We are the lab rats

For many of us, the most personally relevant aspects of psychology are how our minds work in everyday ways. How we learn, how we interpret the world, how we interact with other people and what we are like. To find out about these aspects of the mind, psychologists often perform experiments, either in the laboratory or in the 'field' (out in the world). Or they carry out studies – asking questions or examining statistics, for instance. Only by looking at the behaviour or development of a large number of people can psychologists work out what falls in the middle of the spectrum – what we casually call 'normal'. Some psychology studies focus solely on dysfunctional minds. This is not simply because dysfunctional minds might need special treatment and therapy, but because they can help to shed light on 'normal' minds.

BEHIND THE MASK

To many people, mental illness is more frightening than physical illness. We can't see what's going on. There's no rash or twisted limb to look at, so we can't imagine what the problem is or how severe it is. Many people feel threatened by any type of mental illness, even though someone with (say) OCD or depression is no threat to anyone else. We can't catch the illness, like we can catch flu.

As we start to understand how problems with the brain can cause some types of psychological conditions, perhaps people will become less worried. After all, producing too little dopamine in the brain (associated with depression and Alzheimer's disease, among other conditions) is not conceptually any different from producing too little insulin in the pancreas (which causes type 1 diabetes).

Hard work

Psychological studies are plagued with problems. If people know their behaviour is being investigated, they often change it. They might do this for various reasons: to please the experimenter, to seem like the kind of person they would like to be, to be perverse or, perhaps unconsciously, because the alien situation of the laboratory set-up makes them anxious. This means that many studies have had to be surreptitious, and that raises ethical problems. Some of the landmark experiments in psychology would not be allowed by an ethics committee today. Many of the subjects didn't give consent for what was going to happen to them. And some experiments risked causing genuine psychological harm to the people selected – encouraging them to act in ways they would later regret, for example. Later on, we will look at some examples of psychology experiments that had potentially damaging effects on their subjects.

Like-minded?

It's hard to say how far the results of a study can be extended to the general population, particularly to those of different cultures. The subjects are often of a certain type – people who readily agree or volunteer to be involved in experiments – and therefore they are not necessarily typical of the population at large.

Subjects are sometimes chosen from an even more specific group of people; they may be students who are short of cash and therefore willing to take part in an experiment for the money. How far can results gleaned from studying affluent 21-year-old American college students (for example) be extended to explain the behaviour of elderly Afghani goat-keepers, workers in a Bangladeshi garment factory, Tibetan nuns, or Brazilian business tycoons?

New approaches

Typically, psychology looks at our emotional state and behaviour. In the past, psychologists could only come to conclusions about how our minds work by paying heed to what we say and do. The physical structure of the brain was the realm of neurologists. But today, psychologists can also see the mind in action by using various scanning technologies to reveal what the brain is doing at certain times and when we feel certain moods. As a result, neurology and psychology are coming closer together, and even undertaking some joint ventures.

So that's where we will start – with what we can learn from a brain.

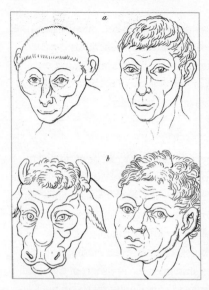

Left: Physiognomic comparisons of a man and a monkey, and a man and a bull. The belief that an individual's inner character could be read in their outward appearance ('physiognomy') was popular during the 18th and 19th centuries. Many writers of the period, such as Charles Dickens and Edgar Allan Poe, included physiognomic descriptions of characters in their work.

Burning questions

There are two very big, over-arching questions in psychology that stray into the realms of philosophy, evolutionary biology and jurisprudence. The first: to what extent is the mind the product of nature (our biological inheritance), or the result of nurture (our environment and upbringing)? The second: to what extent can we be said to have free will and, consequently, be held responsible for our own actions? The two questions overlap.

Some of the questions asked in this book deal with aspects of how much of our psychological make-up is hardwired and how much comes from the environment. Chapter 7 – *Is morality natural?* and Chapter 18 – *What do you see?* both touch on this. It seems that the basic structure of the brain gives us certain intrinsic gifts, such as an ability to learn language and the ability to interpret what we see. These are abilities that each new human being does not need to learn from scratch. In other ways, we are the product of our environment. Chapter 6 – *Does attention spoil a baby?* and Chapter 17 – *Can you spot a psychopath?*

both touch on how upbringing can affect a person's mental health in later life.

If a lot of our behaviour is determined by brain chemistry or structure, or factors in early childhood over which we had no control, can we be held responsible for what we do? Many legal systems provide for people being less responsible if deemed mentally impaired, but this is quite a specific defence. The psychopath with the combination of brain structure and upbringing which makes it almost inevitable that he will kill will still be locked up for murder. Recently, psychology has gone even

IS FREE WILL AN ILLUSION?

Studies of the brain have shown that when we think we are making a free choice, our brain has already started acting. In a neurology experiment conducted in 2008, researchers used a brain scanner to measure the brain activity of subjects who were choosing whether to press a button with their left or right hand. They discovered that the brain fired the associated neurons several seconds before the subjects thought they had decided.

Other experiments have found similar results. When brain scanners are used to monitor people who believe they are freely choosing to move parts of their body, the area of the brain that is preparing the movement is active for around a second before the person moves. The conscious intention to move and the movement itself happen at virtually the same time. It appears that if we have free will at all, it isn't where we think it is. The feeling of deciding to move is our interpretation of something that has already happened in the brain. Some other part of the brain, of which we are unaware, has apparently decided on the movement and started it off. Then we get the feeling 'Ooh, I know, I'll move my hand,' by which time it's already happening.

further in undermining free will – the entire construct might be an illusion (see the box on the previous page). If people are doomed to follow certain paths, the issues of reward and punishment become quite complex.

Don't try this at home

The questions posed here are not, on the whole, related to mental disorders and the answers suggested are not intended to be prescriptive. Please don't use this book to try to diagnose any mental problems in yourself or others. The book aims to take a peek at how the mind works, but it doesn't give definitive answers and it can't begin to cover all the approaches psychologists have taken. In the same vein, please don't try reproducing any of the experiments described.

CHAPTER 1

What can we learn from a brain?

We can't watch the brain working,
so how do we know what it does?

Psychology is the study of what goes on in the brain – thinking, learning, personality, dreams, desires, character formation, behaviour determination, and disorders of all of those. But unlike the study of what goes on in, say, the heart, there is no mechanical process to observe directly. So scientists have had to find some ingenious ways of monitoring our thought processes.

Viewing our thoughts

In the early days of psychology, the only way of looking at a brain directly was once its owner had died. All psychological study had to be through experimenting with, observing and questioning live brain-users. While all those techniques remain extremely useful today, we now have ways of viewing the living brain while it's doing its stuff. But viewing the brain raises as many questions as it answers. Knowing about the biology of the brain only takes us so far. We can see it is doing something, but we still can't see quite what it is, or how it is doing it. We can see neurons firing as someone thinks, but we can't see what they are thinking, or why they had that thought, or how they will remember (or forget) it.

SIZE MATTERS

Animal	Neurons	Animal	Neurons
Fruit fly	100,000	Cockroach	1,000,000
Mouse	75,000,000	Cat	1,000,000,000
Baboon	14,000,000,000	Human	86,000,000,000

What goes where?

For millennia, the only way to discover which parts of the brain were used for different functions was to observe people who had suffered head injuries and note how this had affected their mental or physical abilities, mood or behaviour. The changes were a good indication that different parts of the brain were responsible for different functions (emotions, cognition, personality and so on). Post-mortem examination revealed brain damage that might have been related to changes or impaired function that had been noticed in the person when they were alive. To acquire meaningful insights into the workings of the brain, scientists needed lots of brains to examine, and sophisticated scientific equipment to do it with. So the brain was pretty much a closed book until the 20th century. It's not a very open book, even now.

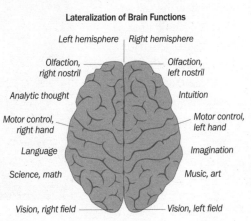

Lateralization of Brain Functions

Left hemisphere   Right hemisphere

Olfaction, right nostril — Olfaction, left nostril

Analytic thought — Intuition

Motor control, right hand — Motor control, left hand

Language — Imagination

Science, math — Music, art

Vision, right field — Vision, left field

The unfortunate Phineas Gage

The idea that specific parts of the brain might be responsible for different functions originated with the medical case of a railroad construction foreman called Phineas Gage. On 13 September 1848, Gage was seriously injured when a metal tamping iron, a long, pointed rod weighing six kilograms, was accidentally fired through his head. It entered through the cheek and left through the top of his head, taking fragments of his brain with it. He lost a bit more brain when he vomited, and 'about half a teacup full' of brain fell on the floor, according to the doctor who attended him. The main damage was to one of the frontal lobes of his brain.

Although his friends had a coffin ready and waiting for him, remarkably, Gage lived. But his personality changed considerably for a long period. Instead of the polite, friendly man he had been before the accident, he became difficult and antisocial (though not the terrible character that legend suggests). His social ineptitude lessened with time, and he ended his days working as a stagecoach driver in Chile. It's possible that the routine of his new life helped in his rehabilitation, as structured activity is found to be helpful in the treatment of many patients suffering damage to the frontal lobes.

Phineas Gage

In two minds

The brain comprises two halves, or hemispheres. Each hemisphere contains the same structures and there is communication between the two via a thick bundle of nerve fibres called the *corpus callosum*.

How the two hemispheres work together was explained by Roger W. Sperry, a neuropsychologist who used the technique of severing the *corpus callosum* to treat patients with severe epilepsy. It sounds drastic, and it was, but it did cure the epilepsy. After he had cut the connection between the two hemispheres, the right hand literally did not know what the left hand was doing.

At first the surgery appeared to have little impact on the patients – apart from relieving their epilepsy. But investigation of Sperry's split-brain patients soon revealed that there had been other major changes. In the process, Sperry gained new insights into how the two halves of the brain normally work together.

Sperry found that if he presented a picture to the right visual field (processed by the left side of the brain), the patient could name the object in speech or writing, but if it was presented to the left visual field they could not. They could, though, identify the object by pointing. From this, Sperry concluded that language is processed in the left side of the brain.

He found, too, that objects shown to the left side of the brain can only be recognized by that side. If he displayed different symbols in the right and left visual fields and then asked the person to draw what they saw, they only drew the symbol shown in the left visual field. If he then asked them what they had drawn (not seen), they described the symbol in the right visual field. Objects originally viewed in the left visual field were recognized if viewed again in the left, but not if then viewed in the right visual field.

Look inside

Today, there are various ways we can examine brain structure and activity:

- A computed tomography (CT) scan uses X-rays and a computer to produce three-dimensional images of the brain. It shows the normal structure and can highlight damage, tumours and other structural changes or abnormalities.

- An electroencephalogram (EEG) monitors the electrical impulses produced by brain activity. It can reveal the person's state of arousal (sleeping, waking, and so on) and show how long it takes for a stimulus to trigger brain activity or reveal the areas where brain activity takes place when the subject performs an action or is exposed to a stimulus.

- A positron emission tomography (PET) scan reveals the real-time activity of the brain by showing where radioactively-tagged oxygen or glucose is being concentrated. This is because the harder the brain works, the more oxygen and glucose it uses. It's useful for seeing which parts of the brain are used for specific tasks or functions.

- Magnetic resonance imaging (MRI) combines radio waves with a powerful magnetic field to detect different types of tissue, and produces detailed anatomical images of the brain.

- Magnetoencephalography (MEG) picks up the tiny magnetic signals produced by neural activity. This is currently expensive and not widely used, but it provides the most detailed real-time indication of brain function.

> *'[Each hemisphere is] indeed a conscious system in its own right, perceiving, thinking, remembering, reasoning, willing, and emoting, all at a characteristically human level, and . . . both the left and the right hemisphere may be conscious simultaneously in different, even in mutually conflicting, mental experiences that run along in parallel.'*
>
> Roger Wolcott Sperry, 1974

For the first time, brain scans show psychologists which parts of the brain are involved in different types of activity and behaviour. Comparing brain scans of psychopathic killers, for instance, shows that they all have similar brain abnormalities (see Chapter 17).

DO YOU ONLY USE 10 PER CENT OF YOUR BRAIN?

Another popular psychology myth is that we only use 10 per cent of our brain. In fact, we use all of our brain, though not at the same time. Many of us don't use our brain to its full potential most of the time, but all areas of the brain have a function and we do use those functions during the course of a day or a week.

You can always do more – when you learn new skills, your brain makes new connections between neurons to store knowledge and patterns of behaviour.

Knowledge and growth

In 2000, Eleanor Maguire at University College, London, used MRI scanning to compare the brains of London taxi drivers with those of a control group of men of similar age and profile. The taxi drivers had spent up to four years memorizing routes through the 25,000 streets of London; this is known colloquially as the 'Knowledge'.

Maguire's study showed that the posterior hippocampus of a taxi driver's brain is significantly larger than the hippocampus in members of the control group. This research not only indicated the importance of the hippocampus in navigation and spatial awareness, but also demonstrated that the brain (or at least the hippocampus) can adapt with regular use, building up like a muscle that strengthens with repeated exercise.

The longer the men had worked as taxi drivers, the more marked the difference. In a follow-up study, Maguire found that the size of the hippocampus decreased to normal in the brains of retired taxi drivers who were no longer using the Knowledge and therefore not needing to exercise the hippocampus so much.

LEFT BRAIN, RIGHT BRAIN?

In popular psychology, it's common to refer to 'left brain' and 'right brain' functions or personalities. If the left half of your brain is dominant (or so the story goes), you will be good at logical and analytical thought and be more objective than a right-brain thinker. If the right half of the brain is in charge, you'll be intuitive, creative, thoughtful and subjective. But almost all functions are carried out approximately equally by both halves of the brain. Where there are differences, there's a variance between individuals as to which hemisphere does more of one thing or another.

The only area of significant difference is in language processing, as discovered by Sperry. The left hemisphere works at the syntax and meaning of language, while the right hemisphere is better at the emotional content and nuance of language.

Maguire used a computer game which involved navigating around London to watch the taxi drivers' brains in action. She found that the hippocampus was most active at the start of the task, when the driver had to think about and plan the route. Maguire's study was important in showing which area of the brain is used for navigation, and how the brain can adapt with increased stimuli – an ability that holds promise for people who have suffered brain damage and require rehabilitation.

Brains in jars

Long before we had modern imaging technologies, scientists supposed that if they were able to look at someone's brain, they would be able to see physical differences between, for instance, very bright people and those of average intelligence, or between violent criminals and law-abiding citizens. But it didn't turn out to be that simple. For example, intelligent people don't have larger brains, as we might expect.

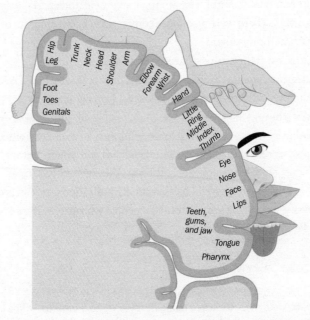

This diagram shows which areas of the brain correspond to sensory input from different parts of the body. The relative size of the various body parts shows how much of the brain is involved in processing the signals it receives, so the hand is much larger than the foot in this image.

When Albert Einstein died in 1955, his brain was removed, examined, photographed and stored; then it disappeared for 20 years until it was rediscovered in 1978. The brain had been cut into 240 pieces for microscopic examination. There was no size difference between Einstein's brain and 'normal' brains (that is, brains of those who were not Nobel prize-winning physicists), but there were some structural differences. Einstein's brain lacks a few of the features found in normal brains, and it's been suggested that this may have helped it make neural connections more easily. The inferior parietal lobe of Einstein's brain was 15 per cent wider than other brains; this area is used for mathematical thought, visualizing movement and spatial-visual cognition. There were also more connections between parts of his brain than is usual.

Looking at the brains of dead people also helps us to understand mental illness. The brains of people who had Alzheimer's disease show tissue loss and shrinkage.

With brain scans, we can see when people are thinking or dreaming, which part of the brain works on different activities and whether there are brain abnormalities or damage. But we can't yet see *what* people are thinking. Although seeing the thoughts of others would have serious implications for personal privacy, it could be very helpful for people who are paralyzed and unable to communicate.

JUST THINK!

Brain-computer interface (BCI) devices pick up brainwaves and feed them directly into a computer. Using such devices, it has been possible to train macaque monkeys to move things using only their thoughts. In these experiments, the monkey's arms were restrained and a sensor the width of a hair was implanted in its brain. This detected the signals that would normally go to the monkey's arm and used them to control a robotic arm instead. This system is not yet regarded as safe for humans.

Mind and body – who's boss?

Descartes struggled with the problem of how the mind and body could interact – of how the mental intention to lift a hand could be translated into the action itself. In fact, the brain seems to have far more sway over the body than that.

One of the strangest mental disorders is the rare Cotard's syndrome. Sufferers of this terrible condition believe that they are dead. Until the advent of brain scans, there was no explanation for how this could come about. But recent research has revealed some clues. It appears that in Cotard's syndrome the link between the senses and the limbic system and amygdalae, responsible for the emotions, is completely lacking. The consequence is that whatever the sufferer sees, hears, smells or touches arouses no emotional response at all. The only way the person can rationalize their complete non-engagement with the world is by concluding that they are dead. Something that seems to be an incontestable proof of madness (not a useful term at the best of times) has a rational basis, with the brain looking at the evidence produced by its damaged self and coming to a conclusion that seems to fit in all ways but one.

Temporary disconnection

According to neuroscientist Vilayanur S. Ramachandran, the extreme feelings of de-personalization and de-realization often experienced by people with depression and anxiety disorders may be caused by a similar mechanism, but on a smaller scale. A temporary disconnection might account for the well-documented phenomenon of people not feeling or being aware of traumatic injury at times of great stress. In an emergency, the amygdalae shut down and the anterior cingulate cortex, located deep in the brain, becomes hyperactive. This structure keeps you alert and helps you make the correct response to a given situation. This trick of the brain is sometimes evident in soldiers in battle who don't feel when a leg is blown off.

In sickness and in health

We have all heard of psychosomatic illness – ill-health for which there is no physical cause. There are many symptoms associated with stress, depression and extreme emotion, including headaches, vomiting, stomach-ache and muscle pains. We are also familiar with the placebo effect of treatments that have no active pharmacological components, but still make people feel better. It is well documented that if people believe they are receiving a potent or effective medicine, they will often get better even if they are only being given sugar pills. Many people suspect that at least some alternative therapies work through the placebo effect – when they work at all.

Perhaps even more surprising and compelling evidence of just how far the brain can control the body comes from the reverse of the placebo effect, called the 'nocebo effect'. This is when illness or even death is triggered by a harmless substance, just because the subject expects there to be a harmful effect. Around 25 per cent of people given a placebo in a drug trial will develop the side effects they were told to expect from the real drug.

. . . especially in sickness

People who die after being cursed are a prime example of the nocebo effect in action. A voodoo practitioner, for example, who believes in the efficacy of a curse, will often die when cursed himself, even though there is no physical reason to do so. Many physicians have noticed that some patients die soon after receiving a negative prognosis, long before they were likely to die from the illness itself. In one case, a young man involved in a drug trial took an overdose (29 capsules) of what he thought was an anti-depressant and became dangerously ill. When he was told he had been in the control group, taking a harmless placebo, he rapidly got better. There have even been suggestions that the health warnings on cigarette packages could make cigarettes more dangerous.

CHAPTER 2

What drives you?

The first aim of the brain is to help you survive. After that, it pursues other needs.

Why do you do the things you do? There are many different motivators. You make breakfast because you are hungry, and go to work because you need the money. But when you have satisfied basic needs, you probably move on to doing things you think will make you happy.

Maslow's pyramid

In 1954, the American psychologist Abraham Maslow published a diagram which he said explained human motivation. The 'pyramid of needs' (see opposite page) shows a hierarchy of needs which must be met. According to Maslow, trying to meet these needs provides the motivation for all human endeavour. When one need has been met, we move on to the next, in order.

Fed and watered

At the bottom of Maslow's pyramid are the most fundamental physical needs – food, water, sleep, air and basic bodily functions (including sex, interestingly). Once these basic needs have been met, people progress to trying to satisfy the need for security. This is not just physical safety, but the feeling of security that comes from having a stable job, a house that won't be repossessed, and a reasonable degree of confidence that you aren't going to drop dead of a heart attack at any minute (as Maslow did).

You and them

The next level of the pyramid moves on to needs that relate more to our place in relation to others. The need for love and belonging is met by having family, friends and sexual intimacy. The next level is the need to be well regarded by others. This is esteem and respect, including self-esteem and confidence. The pinnacle of the pyramid is 'self-actualization', at which point people are fulfilled and have become who they want to be (see Chapter 15).

Although psychologists have largely moved on from Maslow's pyramid, it is still widely referred to in business studies and sociology.

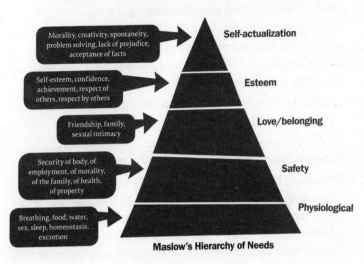

Morality, creativity, spontaneity, problem solving, lack of prejudice, acceptance of facts → **Self-actualization**

Self-esteem, confidence, achievement, respect of others, respect by others → **Esteem**

Friendship, family, sexual intimacy → **Love/belonging**

Security of body, of employment, of morality, of the family, of health, of property → **Safety**

Breathing, food, water, sex, sleep, homeostasis, excretion → **Physiological**

Maslow's Hierarchy of Needs

Acts and motivation

Maslow proposed that this hierarchy of needs motivates human behaviour. If we are hungry, we will seek first of all to eat. If we don't have enough sleep, the need to do so will rule our behaviour as we try to secure time and space to rest. Once one tier of needs is met, we are motivated to satisfy the next tier. Maslow claimed we can't deal with these needs out of sequence – we can only progress to needing, say, job security, once we have enough food and water.

Only when all the lower needs have been met can we look to meet the need for self-actualization. As a consequence, since many people aren't able to meet the lower needs, very few of us – perhaps only 1 or 2 per cent – will ever be self-actualized. That's rather a depressing prospect, which must have disappointed Maslow. But is it true?

What's new?

For millennia, philosophy and religion had pitted the impulses that Maslow identified as higher needs against those he called lower needs. The central dynamic between them was one of conflict, not progression. Maslow was unusual in acknowledging the importance, even primacy, of the needs that exemplars such as Diogenes wanted to deny or suppress. For Maslow, greater things became possible when physical needs were met rather than shunned.

MASLOW'S HUMANISTIC PSYCHOLOGY

Abraham Maslow (1908–70) was born in New York, the youngest of seven children. He was classified as mentally unstable, suffered from anti-Semitic prejudice and bullying, and had a very difficult relationship with a mother he neither liked nor respected. Later, he worked at Columbia University with psychologist Alfred Adler (one of Sigmund Freud's early colleagues), who became a mentor to him. Maslow decided to work on the psychology of the healthy mind, rather than the more common practice of working to understand and remedy disorders of the psyche (psychopathology). He set out to discover what motivates people, and what are the sources and impulses of personal strength and fulfilment – a study he called 'humanistic psychology'.

His work on the hierarchy of needs, self-actualization and peak experiences has been highly influential.

Who, when, where?

Maslow drew up his hierarchy of needs after studying and considering a limited sample of people. The hierarchy is biased towards the concerns of white male Americans. Working from Maslow's rules, Jesus Christ would not have achieved self-actualization – born in a stable to poor parents and committed to chastity, he would have fallen at the first hurdle. More generally, Maslow's hierarchy is not applicable to very different cultures or societies in different times and places. America of the 1950s was an individualistic society. How would his pyramid have fared in a collectivist society, in which people are geared towards not their own personal development but the good of the family group or society as a whole?

NEEDS AND WANTS

The difference between needs and wants is that needs are quantifiable and finite and wants are not. Once our basic needs are met, we can move on to another goal – so once we have enough air, food and water, we don't need lots more. (Although we might like a different type of food, or an extra pudding, we don't need it.) Wants are infinite. We might want a mobile phone; then when we have one we might want a better one, or we might also want a camera or a big car. Wants are insatiable, as there are always more things for us to want.

It is clear that even in an individualistic society some of the needs can be leap-frogged and people can still reach self-actualization. There have been countless creative people who have lived in poverty or sickness, with no social or physical security, who have nevertheless been able to produce wonderful work: Beethoven was deaf, Solzhenitsyn was imprisoned, Marie Curie was dying of radiation sickness and Freddie Mercury was dying from AIDS, to name but a few. Adversities such as these can even be a spur to self-actualization.

Some studies comparing perception of needs in the USA and the Middle East, in wartime and peacetime, threw up significant differences in prioritizing of needs. Some needs also change with age – children prioritize physical needs and the need for love, and adolescents and young adults are more concerned with esteem.

More pyramids or fewer?

Maslow's pyramid was expanded during the 1960s and 1970s to seven or even eight levels. The new levels were cognitive and aesthetic needs, which were slotted in below self-actualization, and transcendence needs (very 1960s), which was placed in the

> ### STOICS AND CYNICS
>
> The philosophical movements of Cynicism and Stoicism, along with some Eastern religions, plot a path to tranquillity, enlightenment and self-actualization that circumvents many of the 'needs' Maslow said had to be met. They tend towards the belief that fulfilment comes from rising above (rather than meeting) needs. The person who can learn to be untroubled by unmet needs will enjoy a more tranquil and satisfying life than one who is always struggling for the next promotion, the bigger TV and the larger expense account.

tier above. Cognitive needs are the requirement for knowledge and meaning; aesthetic needs relate to an appreciation of beauty, form and balance; transcendence concerns the fostering of self-actualization in others.

ERG-onomics

The American psychologist Clayton Paul Alderfer (born 1940) developed Maslow's pyramid slightly differently, categorizing the needs as promoting existence, relatedness and growth (ERG). Alderfer believed that the lowest level in Maslow's scheme related to physical 'existence'. He classified the needs which concerned a place in society and relationships with others as 'relatedness'. The need for self-esteem and self-actualization he labelled 'growth'.

Alderfer made a place in his scheme for regression. If a higher-level need is not met, the individual will slip down the ladder and redouble their efforts at a lower need in the hope of satisfying a higher need. We can see this every day in people who think they will be satisfied and happy if they earn more and spend more on assorted 'stuff'. The attempt to fulfil spiritual needs through the acquisition of physical goods is doomed to failure.

It's all good

While some psychologists were shoe-horning new tiers into Maslow's pyramid, others were keen to demolish it. In its place came systems that proposed a more horizontal plane of needs. Chilean-born German economist and environmentalist Manfred Max-Neef has proposed a taxonomy of human needs that he sees as inter-related and interdependent. He classifies human needs as the following:

- subsistence • protection • affection • understanding
- participation • leisure • creation • identity • freedom

By fitting them into categories of being (qualities), having (things), doing (actions) and interacting (settings), he developed a matrix of 36 items.

SEX AND VIOLENCE HELD IN CHECK

Sigmund Freud, the father of psychoanalysis, divided the psyche into three levels: the id, the ego and the super-ego. The id was unrestrained instincts, passions and hungers. It was kept in order by the ego, which negotiated the id's way through the world to avoid too much conflict. The super-ego was something like the conscience and could prevent some of the more outlandish promptings of the id coming to fruition. The id, then, is the main motivating force and the ego and super-ego keep it in check.

These fundamental human needs don't have to be satisfied in any particular order, and the satisfaction of some will go some way towards the satisfaction of others. They don't form a hierarchy, but for a society to flourish people have to feel all these needs are being met. Satisfying them gives a community a way of identifying and measuring its 'wealths' and 'poverties'.

MEETING NEEDS

Max-Neef went on to classify six types of 'satisfier' or methods of meeting (or failing to meet) needs. These are:

- **Violators:** these claim to satisfy a need, but make the situation worse. An example would be carrying a weapon to satisfy a need for personal security.
- **Pseudo-satisfiers:** these claim to satisfy a need, but have little or no real effect. An example might be wearing designer clothes to give yourself a sense of identity, whereas the identity belongs to the clothes, not to you.
- **Inhibiting satisfiers:** these over-satisfy one need, and consequently make it harder to satisfy other needs. If parents are overprotective, for instance, they can make it difficult for their child to develop identity, understanding and affection.
- **Singular satisfiers:** these satisfy a single need and have no impact on others. For example, providing food assistance to people who are hungry helps to satisfy their need for food, but doesn't address the need for housing or heating or improve their future prospects for food security.
- **Synergistic satisfiers:** these satisfy a specific need and also help to meet other needs. For example, providing nutritious school meals gives a child food, but also helps to build knowledge about healthy eating and nurtures a sense of community.

CHAPTER 3

Don't you have a mind of your own?

You know what you think, don't you? It's surprising how easy it is to persuade people to change their ideas.

Imagine this: you're watching a TV talent show and everyone else is rooting for a performer you dislike. Are you going to buck the trend and criticize the favourite? Or will you go with the flow, and maybe even decide the guy's not so bad really? After all, if your friends like his act, perhaps you're missing something . . . .

Psychology experiments suggest we are less resistant to the pressure to conform than we might believe. We will go along with other people's views even when there is no material cost in not conforming. So just why are you putty in their hands?

The Asch conformity experiment

In 1951, the Polish-born social psychologist Solomon Asch (1907–96) carried out a groundbreaking experiment in conformity at Swarthmore College, Pennsylvania. In the main part of the experiment, a subject was placed with seven people who were presented as volunteers, but were actually confederates of Asch who were working to an agreed script.

The group was shown two cards. One displayed a single line. The other showed three lines of differing lengths, one of which matched the line on the first card. The group was asked to say which of the three lines, labelled A, B and C, matched the single line. This test was repeated many times. For the first set of trials, Asch's confederates gave the correct answer. Thereafter, they all gave the same wrong answer. All the confederates gave their answers first. Asch was interested to see whether the volunteers would be swayed by the wrong answers given by others.

In a control experiment, a volunteer had to give answers without other people being present and therefore with no pressure to conform. In the control, the volunteer gave an incorrect answer less than 1 per cent of the time. This showed that the task was not especially difficult.

In the genuine trials, when the confederates gave the wrong answer, the volunteers also gave wrong answers 33 per cent of the time; and 75 per cent of the volunteers gave a wrong answer at least once. Afterwards Asch interviewed the participants and described the true nature of the experiment, noting how they explained their behaviour.

Along the right lines?

People who conformed to the group answer, whether or not it was correct, might have:

- believed that the incorrect answer was true (relatively few fell into this group)
- reached a point where they realized that they must be wrong, because everyone else had agreed on a different answer ('distortion of judgement')
- realized that everyone else was giving the wrong answer, but agreed with it to avoid being the odd one out or looking inferior ('distortion of action')

More people decided that they must be wrong if everyone else agreed on a different answer. This put them in the 'distortion of judgement' group.

Among those who did not conform, people might:

- act confidently in disagreeing, even though they felt some conflict
- act in a withdrawn way, with no conflict
- show doubt, but still give the answer they thought was true as they felt the need to do the task properly

Join the club – for a while

In variations on his experiment, Asch discovered that there was less conformity if one other person gave the correct response, or if subjects were allowed to record their response in writing

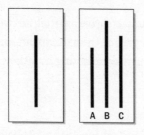

Subjects in Asch's experiment had to say which line on the right-hand card matched the line on the left-hand card.

rather than say it out loud. This suggests they didn't want to look foolish to the other participants by giving the 'wrong' answer, so they went along with it rather than struggling to know the answer or disagreeing with the majority verdict.

Asch cited his results as evidence of normative social influence; that is, people tend to conform publicly to the majority decision or view in order to be accepted by the group, even though they might privately disagree with it. But social psychologist John Turner argued that the participants revealed in the interviews that they did have genuine uncertainty about the correct answer. The answer might have been obvious to the researchers, but it was not necessarily so to the participants (though looking at the cards it's hard to see how people could have genuinely got the answer wrong). Did they really doubt the answer or were they trying to persuade themselves that they did, preferring to see themselves as poor at comparing lines rather than conforming to a bad decision? Turner developed self-categorization theory, which deals with how we see ourselves and how we interpret our own actions.

Peer pressure

Asch's experiment dealt with peer pressure. This is the pressure we all feel to conform to the norms in our social group. It's not just advertising that makes you buy a particular brand of smart phone or trainers. You are also swayed if people around you have them. If all those discerning people – in the social group you respect, belong to, or aspire to join – chose a particular product, surely they must be right? Peer pressure is supposed to explain why young people take up smoking or become involved in underage sex or cyberbullying.

Advertisers promote an image of successful/attractive/intelligent people, 'like you', buying and using their products so even if the people around you aren't using them, you will consider yourself an outsider unless you conform. You're an attractive, intelligent person, aren't you? So why don't you have the watch, mobile phone or car that is the badge of your tribe? It takes some self-confidence to buy a cheap, inelegant mobile phone when everyone else you know owns the latest sleek model. Peer pressure is harnessed deliberately and cynically in other areas of life, too. Employers hold bonding exercises such as weekend survival camps, parties and other social events to foster the belief in employees that they are among friends, not just work colleagues. If you feel you belong to a group in which the other members turn up early and work hard, it's likely that you will do the same.

No big deal

The Asch experiment wasn't sinister. It didn't require participants to do anything immoral or even particularly uncomfortable.

WHO'S PRESSURING WHOM?

When we think of peer pressure, we tend to imagine 'peers' putting pressure on someone to do something – smoke a cigarette, for instance, or drink alcohol. That does happen, but more often the pressure comes from ourselves. We want to be part of the group that does dangerous stunts or takes party drugs because those people are cool and we want to be seen as cool and to see ourselves as cool. Internal pressure is more compelling than external pressure – and potentially much more dangerous.

The worst a non-conformist could expect was ridicule from people he didn't know, and the worst a conformist could experience was embarrassment when the true nature of the experiment was revealed. But it's easy to underestimate the power of peer pressure. How far will people go in order to conform, to be part of a tribe? It seems that they will do things they would previously have considered unthinkable.

The Third Wave

In 1967, in Palo Alto, California, history teacher Ron Jones was having difficulty persuading his high school students of the ease and speed with which fascism took root in Nazi Germany. To their credit, the students found it hard to believe that ordinary, intelligent German citizens had bought into an ideology which led to the gas chambers and the desire for a 10,000-year Reich. To prove his point, Jones abandoned his usual teaching methods.

He invented a movement, which he called the Third Wave, and told his students that its aim was to overthrow democracy. You might think this would alienate the students, but Jones made a convincing case in its defence, saying it would deliver a higher standard of performance and greater rewards for individuals. The problem with democracy, he said, was that it focused on the individual and reduced the strength of the group.

A slippery slope

On the first day of his experiment, Jones insisted that students stand up to ask or answer a question; he told them to open each remark by addressing him as 'Mr Jones', made them sit according to a seating plan and enforced strict discipline in class. Acting as an authoritarian figure, he improved the efficiency of the class considerably. Originally he had intended to stop the experiment after the first day. But it was going well, so he took it a bit further.

The second day, he introduced a salute and demanded that students greet one another with it even outside class. They all complied. The group developed quite astonishing coherence and self-discipline. People like to belong, and the more special the belonging seems, the more they want it. By the third day, the 'movement' had spread beyond the history class, with other students asking to join. The academic performance and motivation of all members improved dramatically. Jones assigned members individual tasks, such as designing a banner, and showed them how to initiate new members. He told them to exclude non-members from his classroom. By the end of the third day, there were 200 members (it had started with only the 30 members of Jones' class). Some members spontaneously started reporting any students who breached the many rules. It had become a self-policing movement.

> **'Strength through discipline, strength through community, strength through action, strength through pride.'**
>
> The motto of Jones' Third Wave group

All the way down

By the fourth day, Jones felt that the experiment was getting out of hand and decided to end it. He told all the members that the movement was part of a national movement which would be announced the next day, and they were to attend a rally at noon to watch a broadcast by the movement's presidential candidate. When the students turned up for the rally, Jones told them that they had been part of an experiment in fascism and had all willingly – and rapidly – welded themselves into a group convinced of their own superiority. Then he showed them a film about Nazi Germany.

So who do you think you are?

According to psychologist Wendy Treynor, the 'identity shift effect' is at work when we give in to peer pressure. To start with, we fear social rejection if our behaviour doesn't match the standard behaviour of the group. When we adjust our behaviour to fit in, we feel uncomfortable because our behaviour now doesn't match our own beliefs or standards. This is cognitive dissonance (see Chapter 24). To resolve the internal conflict, we adjust our standards to match those we have recently adopted. This returns us to the harmonious state of no conflict, either internal or external, and the happy state of fitting in with our peers. Everyone is happy; and sometimes they are happy Nazis.

CHAPTER 4

All for one or one for all?

Are people just naturally selfish or naturally generous? Or is generosity another form of selfishness?

If left to our own devices, would we all be kind to one another or would we be brutish and selfish? Biology, and the principle of the selfish gene, could argue it either way – it's good for you, as an individual, to further your own cause and that of your family (your genes); but for the species as a whole it's better if we are altruistic and cooperative.

Wild humans

If we were able to investigate humans 'in the wild', we could examine innate behaviour without the crust of social niceties that has been laid down over millennia. But we can't, and even 20th-century anthropologists who studied non-industrialized societies were still looking at them with rules that either reinforced or obscured what might be natural behaviour. Nevertheless, humans are animals, and we can look at other animals to see whether empathy and selflessness are naturally occurring traits. If other animals are naturally helpful, even altruistic, perhaps it follows that people are too.

Are rats kinder than you?

We tend to think of rats as dirty, disease-carrying and vicious. But they are (also) smart and altruistic. A study in 1958 found that if pressing a lever to get food gave an electric shock to another rat, then rats would go hungry.

A more sophisticated study in 1967 explored this further. A cage had two levers for delivering food, one that was easy to operate and one that was very difficult to operate. Sensibly, the rats used the easy one. But when the system was changed so that a second group of rats received an electric shock when the easy lever was used, the rats cooperated to work the difficult lever.

In 2011, a study in Chicago found that altruism in rats went even further. Offered the choice of operating a lever to free a trapped rat or to access chocolate, the rats freed the trapped rat. They then shared the chocolate with the escapee. The rats could have eaten the chocolate first and then freed the other rat, but they chose the sharing option.

KICKED OUT OF THE CAVE?

If humans naturally had an 'one for all' attitude, we would expect that individuals no longer useful to the group would be excluded from societies with scarce resources. Yet evidence of where an 'all for one' attitude has prevailed suggests that this is not the case. Remains of prehistoric cave dwellers have been found with signs of severe injuries or disabilities which would have prevented them from gathering or preparing food, or performing other essential tasks. Some of these people have clearly been cared for into old age, or for a considerable time after their disability occurred.

A man in his twenties, buried in North Vietnam 4,000 years ago, had severe disabilities caused by a genetic condition which would have started in adolescence. The fact that he survived for ten years into adulthood proved that others had cared for him. The 45,000-year-old skeleton of a severely disabled man found in Iraq, and the skull of a brain-damaged child who lived in Spain 530,000 years ago, also show that 'care in the community' goes back a very long way.

The skeleton of a disabled prehistoric man found in North Vietnam. Archaeologists have concluded that he would have had little, if any, use of his arms and would have been unable to feed himself. He could only have survived into adulthood by being cared for by other members of his community.

Is altruism good for you?

Monkeys spend a lot of time grooming one another. This apparent act of kindness has obvious benefits for the community. It helps to build bonds between individuals, making the community stronger. It reduces the parasite population, making the community healthier and benefiting each individual. But there is more to it than that.

Some scientists have suggested that altruism in animals (and humans) can make an individual look attractive to a mate. Not only are they kind, they have resources to spare. A partner with time to spare to groom his siblings must be good at finding food.

Stuart Semple of Roehampton University, London, studied grooming and stress in Barbary macaque monkeys. He found that monkeys who groom others have lower stress levels than those who don't. It's not certain whether already laid-back and stress-free monkeys are more likely to groom their neighbours, or whether the grooming produces more laid-back and stress-free monkeys – the cause and effect in this study requires further research.

> 'She is such a good friend that she would throw all her acquaintances into the water for the pleasure of fishing them out again.'
>
> Charles Maurice de Talleyrand (1754–1838)

CHAPTER 5

Who cares what celebrities think?

Just because a person can sing doesn't mean they understand politics.

Singers are famous and successful because they can sing well, actors because they can act well, sportspeople because they can play sport well and models because they are good-looking. If you want an example of how to sing, act, play sport or look good, you can't beat them. But why should we be interested in what they think about politics, charity, child-rearing, dieting, cooking or any of the other issues so many of them dabble in or pronounce upon?

Our fascination with celebrity opinion and life choices is called the 'halo effect'.

He seems a nice man . . .

In 1920, American psychologist Edward Thorndike published his findings on how commanding officers rated the soldiers in their charge. The COs had to assess their men on physical qualities (such as neatness, voice and bearing), intellect, leadership skills, and personal qualities (including dependability, loyalty and selflessness). The officers tended to find their soldiers either good across the board or pretty bad at just about everything. There were not many instances of COs rating soldiers well for some attributes and badly for others.

It seems we have a tendency to generalize from one attribute to others, so a positive opinion of someone is likely to extend to all areas of their personality. Conversely, if we take against someone, we will assume that they are bad through and through. This not only includes related traits (if someone is mean and selfish, it might seem reasonable to assume they will be unhelpful and stingy) but it extends to unrelated aspects (such as assuming that, as they are selfish, they are also lacking in intelligence). It's a tendency that can even mix physical and psychological attributes. For example, disliking someone's voice or accent, or finding them either physically attractive or repellent, can affect how we view their character.

Would you buy underwear from David Beckham?

Advertisers exploit the halo effect when they use celebrities to endorse their products. Some endorsements make sense: if a successful athlete advertises running shoes there is good reason to suppose he might know a good running shoe when he sees one. (Though it's more likely he just knows a good million dollars when he sees it.) But why would we be likely to share his taste in, say, underwear?

Similarly, why would we believe a beautiful young model, too young to have wrinkles, when she endorses a wrinkle cream?

VOTE REAGAN – BUT WHY?

Actors sometimes become politicians. Some actors are genuinely intelligent people and make good politicians; but this isn't always the case. During his time in office as US president, Ronald Reagan was mocked for his apparent stupidity and laziness; he was caught sleeping through important conferences, and recorded giving information that was so inaccurate it was laughable. These traits were evident when he was governor of California, but he was still nominated and voted in as US president. Why? Because people liked his films, his familiarity and his manner – so they assumed he would be a good president. As it turned out, under Reagan the US enjoyed a period of economic prosperity and national security with low unemployment; it also saw the end of the Cold War.

Advertisers always work on aspiration and association – we see an attractive person using a particular product in a glamorous setting and we buy into the implication that some of the glamour will rub off on us if we use the same product. Celebrity endorsement goes further than that, though, in that it trades on our subconscious assumption that if someone is good at singing/acting/kicking a ball, they will also have sound judgement when it comes to choosing breakfast cereal or cars or underwear.

The good impression created by the product's association with the celebrity is 'sticky' – this means we will remember it even if we know nothing else about the product, and therefore be more likely to choose it. Of course, the opposite is also true – if we dislike the celebrity, we will be less likely to choose the product. That's why only physically attractive and inoffensive celebrities are generally chosen to appear in advertisements and why advertisers are quick to drop celebrities who become embroiled in embarrassing scandals.

First impressions count

First impressions are notoriously difficult to change. If you make a bad impression the first time you meet someone, it's hard to get them to think well of you. And if you like someone straight away, they will have to do something seriously wrong before you turn against them.

We don't like being wrong or admitting that we're wrong. And revising our first impressions involves admitting to ourselves that we were wrong in our initial assessment. We'd actually prefer to spend time with someone we now know is not very nice than admit we were wrong in judging them to be nice in the first place. The more time and emotional energy we invest in someone, the harder it is to admit that we were wrong about them.

He couldn't have done it

When a celebrity is accused of a horrible crime, there is often a knee-jerk reaction among the public to denounce the denouncement. But a lot depends on the celebrity's public image. When the movie director Woody Allen was accused of abuse by his adopted daughter in 2014, many people with no personal knowledge of the individuals or the case leapt to conclusions about his innocence or guilt. Those who assumed his daughter was lying based their view on their admiration for him as a film director. Many other people assumed he was guilty, for equally unfounded reasons.

The same assumptions protect many people in high office and positions of public trust. Just because someone has a good political brain doesn't mean that he or she will be moral in their sexual behaviour, honest in their dealings with their employees or kind to their children.

The word of a non-famous person (such as one of the children abused by the British television presenter Jimmy Savile) carries little weight with the public and is less likely to be believed.

> '**In one study, men who saw a new-car ad that included a seductive young woman model rated the car as faster, more appealing, more expensive-looking, and better designed than did men who viewed the same ad without the model. Yet when asked later, the men refused to believe that the presence of the young woman had influenced their judgements.**'
>
> Robert Cialdini, Arizona State University

CAN YOU STILL LIKE THEIR WORK?

Eric Gill, a brilliant artist, sexually abused his own children, had an incestuous relationship with his sister and had sex with his dog. Film director Roman Polanski cannot return to the USA as he is still wanted for the rape of a minor. He skipped bail just before sentencing in 1977 and fled to France. The poet Ezra Pound was an anti-Semitic Nazi sympathizer. Composer Richard Wagner was famed for his anti-Semitic views, and Carl Orff was a Nazi sympathizer. Edward Thorndike, who identified the halo effect, was an influential psychologist who promoted eugenics.

Tainted love

It makes us uneasy if we admire the art of creators who have led disreputable personal lives. If we know that an artist abused his wife, was cruel to his children or was racist or fascist, it can make us feel uncomfortable about their work – even if they are dead and not able to benefit from our liking them. It's the opposite of the halo effect: our dislike of one aspect of their personality taints all other aspects.

Pretty and good, or just pretty good?

Physically attractive people have advantages over average-looking people in many areas. They are more likely to get a job, to have favours done for them and even to receive preferential treatment by the legal system if they commit a crime (unless they have used their attractiveness to commit the crime, such as deception). In 2013, Italian researchers submitted fake job applications using a selection of photos of attractive and unattractive people, with identical employment records. The attractive people were more likely to be called for interview than the unattractive people. The average interviewing rate was 30 per cent. Attractive women received interview requests 54 per cent of the time, and attractive men 47 per cent of the time.

On the whole, attractive people earn 10–15 per cent more over their lifetimes than those with average looks. Daniel Hamermesh at the University of Texas has calculated that, for the less-than-average-looking person, this amounts to around $140,000 (£89,000) in lost income. He has proposed that legislation should be brought in to protect the aesthetically challenged from being discriminated against on the grounds of their appearance.

CHAPTER 6

Does attention spoil a baby?

Should you leave a baby to cry or give comfort? Which is better for the child in the long run?

Trends in child development come and go. Sometimes professionals tell parents to leave babies to cry, to avoid giving them too much attention, and to feed them on a strict four-hourly regime. At other times they tell parents to feed on demand, fitting around the baby's sleep patterns, and to engage fully and frequently with the baby with lots of hugs, talking, attention and playing. Is there a right way, or is down to fashion? And can the 'right' way be right for both baby and parent, or is it simply a matter of deciding who to prioritize?

Brutal regime

In the first half of the 20th century, the 'experts' in child psychology and child-rearing were generally of the opinion that childhood and motherly love were unnecessary indulgences. 'We need less sentimentality and more spanking,' said Granville Stanley Hall, pioneer of child psychology and first president of the American Psychological Association. (Despite his credentials, he was a eugenicist who thought no effort should be made to help the physically or mentally ill or disabled, as such distractions were standing in the way of evolution.)

'Less sentimentality and more spanking' was a view shared by many, and parents were generally encouraged to prioritize discipline over affection towards even the youngest children. This was the age in which the wealthy sent their children away to private boarding schools, and when cold showers and a good beating were considered character building. Many parents were emotionally distant – either because they believed it to be beneficial or because they found it convenient.

Attachment theory

It was against this background that British psychologist John Bowlby studied attachment in small children. He collected observational data on institutionalized and delinquent children and on children who had been separated from their parents or orphaned in war. As there were no theories on which to base his conclusions about attachment, Bowlby looked at studies in ethnology, evolution and animal behaviour. He considered Konrad Lorenz's work on imprinting in birds in the 1930s to be highly relevant (see the box on page 56). He developed the theory that there are sound evolutionary reasons for babies to form a close attachment with one individual – usually the mother. The infant has behaviours – crying and smiling, for instance – that encourage the parent to interact. It is the parent's instinct, produced through evolution, to respond to these stimuli from the baby.

'When you are tempted to pet your child, remember that mother love is a dangerous instrument. An instrument which may inflict a never-healing wound, a wound which may make infancy unhappy, adolescence a nightmare, an instrument which may wreck your adult son or daughter's vocational future and their chances for marital happiness.

'Never, never kiss your child. Never hold it in your lap. Never rock its carriage.'

John B. Watson, 1928

In the early 20th century, most children of wealthy families seldom saw their parents. They were cared for by nannies, with whom they often formed a strong bond.

Bowlby suspected that ignoring the stimuli and refusing interaction could do irreparable damage to the child as it prevented the formation of a primary attachment. Children who grow up without a primary attachment can later suffer, he claimed, from delinquency, depression, reduced intelligence and, in the most extreme cases, 'affectionless psychopathy' (meaning that they act without regard for the emotional impact on others).

Critical period

Bowlby believed there was a critical period during which attachment had to be established and maintained. If the child did not form and sustain a bond with a primary care-giver in the first two years of life, it would be unable to do so later on. He said that for these first two years the child should receive continuous care from the primary attachment figure, who was usually the mother (at least in the 1940s and 1950s, when he was carrying out his research). Bowlby's recommendation has implications for children attending day-care or being looked after by other carers. He claimed that the risk from breaking the primary attachment continued until age five, and included separation from and death of the care-giver.

MOTHER GOOSE

The Austrian zoologist Konrad Lorenz (1903–89) studied the 'imprinting' behaviour of newly-hatched greylag geese; this behaviour leads them to form an attachment with the first suitable object they see. In nature, this will be the parent, and the gosling will follow the adult's lead, using visual and auditory stimuli to imitate and thus learn how to become a goose.

Lorenz imprinted goslings on himself (or, rather, his boots – they would follow anyone wearing the boots) and was often followed around by a troupe of goslings.

During the early years, the child learns how to be a person from interaction with the mother or other primary attachment, internalizing a model of how to be in the world. The most important lessons, which will last a lifetime, are that:

- the child is a valuable person
- the child knows that his/her emotional needs will be met
- the child has a 'secure base' for exploring the world

WHO cares

Following his work on attachment in the 1940s, Bowlby was asked by the World Health Organization (WHO) to report on the mental health of homeless children in post-war Europe. His publication, *Maternal Care and Mental Health* (1951), changed the way orphans and displaced children were cared for.

THE '44 THIEVES'

Bowlby conducted a study to test his theory of attachment. He interviewed 44 young people in a child guidance clinic who had been convicted of burglary, and 44 other children (the control group) who were attending the clinic but had no criminal convictions. He found that of the 44 thieves, more than 80 per cent had been separated from their mothers for more than six months during their early life, and more than 30 per cent showed signs of affectionless psychopathy. Of the control group, only a small proportion had been separated from their mothers, and none showed psychopathy.

Critics of the study point out that separation was self-reported and the information could have been inaccurate (though why the subjects should be disbelieved is another moot point). Also, Bowlby conducted the interviews and determined the presence or absence of psychopathy himself, so his interpretation might have been biased in favour of his theory ('experimenter bias').

At the same time, public opinion was undergoing a sea change brought about by the groundbreaking work of Dr Benjamin Spock. *The Common Sense Book of Baby and Child Care* (1946) overturned John B. Watson's behaviourist approach to parenting, and recommended paying attention to children and giving them love and affection. It went on to become a worldwide best-seller, with more than 50 million copies sold.

Today, Dr Spock's advice to feed and comfort babies when they cry seems just plain common sense. And although some of his practical baby-care recommendations have been superseded (the current advice is not to place babies on their stomachs, as he recommends, for example), the emotional and psychological approach is still influential.

Recent interpretations

Few people would now dispute that a child benefits immensely from receiving loving care and attention from at least one stable figure during infancy. But some of the details of Bowlby's conclusions have come under fire.

In talking about 'maternal deprivation', he does not distinguish between deprivation and privation. In deprivation, an attachment is established and then disrupted or removed. In privation, no attachment is formed at all. The latter is far more damaging to the child (see the box on page 62). Bowlby's 'monotropic' assumption that the infant is uniquely attached to a single preferred person, usually the mother, was also called into question by those who believed it undervalued the contribution of fathers and other care-givers. A study in 1964 found that the first significant individual attachment starts around eight months, but others quickly follow. By 18 months of age, many children have two, three, four or more attachments, and only 13 per cent have a single attachment.

Mindful of the requirements of a scientific approach, Bowlby was careful to develop and modify his theories over time.

In a study of privation in 1981, Michael Rutter found that children who had never formed a primary attachment did not show distress when separated from a familiar figure. But subsequently they demonstrated clinging, dependent behaviour, attention-seeking and indiscriminate friendliness, and, later on, an inability to follow rules, form lasting relationships or feel guilt. Rutter argued that this was not solely because of the lack of a mother figure, but was related to factors such as the absence of intellectual stimulation and the social experiences necessary for healthy development.

SPOCK BACKLASH

The world changed during the lifetime of the Spock babies. The sexual permissiveness of the 1960s, the drug-using hippies, the Civil Rights movement, the opposition to the Vietnam War and capitalism, and the rejection of the 1950s *Stepford Wives* lifestyle were all laid at the door of Dr Spock. Did permissive parenting produce the criticized excesses of the 'me' generation?

'The U.S. [paid] the price of two generations that followed the Dr Spock baby plan of instant gratification of needs', wrote Norman Vincent Peale, the best-selling author of *The Power of Positive Thinking*.

Wire mothers and fur mothers

The idea that an infant's primary need is not just nourishment but affectionate physical contact flew in the face of theories of childcare in the 1950s, but was endorsed by later research. American psychologist Harry Harlow carried out an experiment designed specifically to test whether a mother means more to an infant than simply a source of nourishment.

Harlow's experiment would not be allowed now – but it revolutionized views on infancy, parental love and the psychological importance of affection. In 1958, Harlow took new-born rhesus monkeys from their mothers and placed them in cages, in isolation. They could hear and see other young monkeys, but they could not touch or interact with them. Initially, he was just raising the monkeys in the most efficient way for use in the laboratory. But he noticed that those hand-reared without interaction with others were psychologically very different from monkeys reared by their parents. He noticed, too, that in the absence of anything else soft, the babies clung to their cloth nappies. He set out to investigate the role of maternal presence and affection in child development.

MONOTROPY

Monotropy is the attachment of an infant to a single adult, often the mother. It was central to Bowlby's model, but is not characteristic of all child-rearing practice. In Israeli *kibbutzim*, and in some totalitarian regimes and extremist religious groups, close attachment to a parent has been prevented by communal child-rearing. Some of the children raised in this manner have spoken out, declaring the method to be damaging. This is not to say that children cannot be happily reared with more than one strong attachment – two present and involved parents being the obvious model.

Harlow made surrogate monkey mothers from wire and wood. Each baby monkey had its own surrogate mother, and grew attached to it, preferring it to other similar ones. Harlow then created some 'mothers' that were bare wire frameworks and others that were covered with cloth. He put one of each in every baby's cage, with either the cloth mother or the wire-frame mother fitted with a feeding bottle. The baby monkeys all preferred the cloth mothers, whether or not they provided food.

In the cages where the wire mothers provided the milk, babies went to them only to suckle, then returned to the fabric

A CHILD GOES TO HOSPITAL

In the 1950s, Bowlby and his colleague, the social worker James Robertson promoted a film that Robertson made called *A Two-Year-Old Goes to Hospital*. This documented the distress of a child who attended hospital for an operation without her mother. The film prompted a major reform in paediatric care in hospitals and other state institutions.

mothers for comfort. If the baby monkeys were placed in a new environment with their surrogate mothers, they would explore the environment, returning frequently to the fabric mother for comfort. If they were placed alone in the environment, they showed distress (such as curling up and screaming) and did not explore it.

Harlow's conclusion – that nourishment is not the single important aspect of the bond between mother and child – had a revolutionary impact. It supported Bowlby's findings that sustained emotional deprivation in infants could have a lasting negative impact on their development.

A fork in the road

Today, baby-care advice falls into two broad camps. Some professionals want to impose a strict schedule (the Gina Ford 'no nonsense' method encompasses everything from sleeping through the night to potty training). Meantime, the baby-led approach has gone even further towards putting the baby at the centre of his or her own care, with developments such as baby-led weaning, where the child is never fed by a parent or carer but allowed to pick up, drop, throw or play with food at will.

Spock's encouragement to parents to trust and follow their instincts has rather fallen by the wayside as more and more 'experts' vie for the attention of parents, making them feel increasingly anxious about their own abilities.

THE ROMANIAN ORPHANAGE CHILDREN

In Romania, under the regime of Nicolae Ceauşescu, up to 170,000 children were incarcerated in orphanages where they endured neglect and abuse. Many were kept tied to their cots, lying in their own filth, and never picked up or shown affection. After the execution of Ceauşescu in 1989, the plight of these children became known outside Romania and a number of charities moved in to help. Many of the children showed lasting effects from the deprivation they had suffered. Though aged 15, some looked around six or seven years old. Their brains had failed to produce growth hormones and many had impaired intelligence. These were not simply the results of malnutrition, but of being deprived of intellectual stimulation and emotional care. Some of the children who had been taken out of the orphanages at a young age and placed in loving foster homes made good progress, but for many the damage was irreparable.

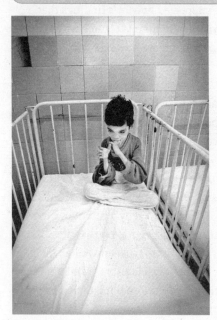

In the 1980s, children in Romanian orphanages suffered neglect and ill-treatment and were found to have no secure attachments with adults. Those who were removed from the orphanages at a young age often recovered, but many children suffered lasting psychological damage.

CHAPTER 7

Is morality natural?

Do even very young children show a sense of morality?

By the time children start school, they have generally developed a rudimentary sense of fairness and justice. They know which actions to classify as nice or nasty (or good or evil). Where do they get this sense from?

Start from home

In their early years, children are exposed to lots of behaviour in the real world, and on television and in the movies. They witness adult responses to their own behaviour and to that of others, and begin to learn what is considered acceptable behaviour and what is unacceptable. But the work of Paul Bloom, a behavioural psychologist at Yale University, Connecticut, suggests that observation and interaction are not the only elements involved.

Bloom has studied morality in babies as young as a few months old and concluded that our morality is not all learned from our dealings with others. His results offer the surprising suggestion that we have an innate moral sense, and this is present even in the smallest infants. That moral sense is fine-tuned as we grow, and is adjusted to suit the society into which we are born.

Moral relativism

Different types of behaviour have a different status in different communities. In the West it is now considered wrong to discriminate against someone on the basis of skin colour, for instance, yet for centuries that was regarded as acceptable behaviour. In Muslim countries, drinking alcohol is considered wrong and is forbidden.

Some societies outlaw homosexuality. In major Western democracies, the act of burning the national flag is considered wrong. Some cultural groups consider it wrong to eat certain types of meat, or certain foods in combination. These types of moral behaviours are culture-specific and must be learned by each citizen.

On the other hand, there is pretty much universal agreement about the morality or immorality of some acts. Most societies consider it wrong to commit murder, to steal from others, and to have sex with close blood relatives.

As these moral strictures crop up in almost all societies, there might be something innate about them – or they might arise again and again because they make societies run smoothly.

> *'Everyone without exception believes his own native customs, and the religion he was brought up in, to be the best.'*
>
> Herodotus, *Histories*, 500BC

Moral babies

Bloom's work with small babies shows, he says, that they exhibit a basic moral sense long before they are old enough to have learned moral lessons by observing other people. Their preferences can be deduced by what they choose to look at and for how long their gaze rests on something.

Helpful and unhelpful shapes

Using this measure, Bloom let babies watch helpful and unhelpful animated shapes and then worked out which they favoured. A red ball was shown struggling to get up a hill. It was then either helped (nudged upwards) by a kindly square, or hindered (its path blocked) by an unhelpful triangle. Bloom switched the shapes around to avoid interference by any preference for one shape over another.

The babies showed a strong preference for the helpful shape. The effect was strengthened if the shapes were given faces. Interestingly, the preference disappeared if the babies didn't first see the ball trying to get up the hill – meaning that the social interaction between the shapes was important, not just the physical movement. Babies as young as three months old preferred to look at the helpful shapes.

The good, the bad, and the indifferent

When Bloom introduced a neutral character, a shape that neither helped nor hindered the hill-climbing ball, babies of six months and older preferred the helpful shape to the neutral shape, and the neutral shape to the hindering shape. Babies of three months old didn't distinguish between helpful and neutral, but still disliked the hindering shape. This is in keeping with the 'negativity bias' common in adults and children – we have a greater sensitivity to bad stuff than to good stuff, and are more likely to respond to something negative than to something positive. We will complain about someone who does an unkind or outrageous act, but few of us will applaud someone who does a kindly act.

Bloom concluded that babies can recognize considerate and inconsiderate behaviour very early on in their development – probably before they can be said to have learned it, as they won't have been exposed to clear models. He suggests this indicates an innate moral sense, with the brain primed with a simple sense of morality right from the start.

Play nicely

Karen Wyn, also at Yale, carried out another experiment, this time with one-year-olds. The children watched a puppet show in which two puppets were playing cooperatively; suddenly a third puppet snatched the ball they were playing with and ran off. The children were then shown the puppets, with a reward in front of each, and asked to remove the reward from one of them. Most toddlers removed the reward from the 'naughty' puppet. One boy not only removed the reward, but hit the 'naughty' puppet. This experiment adds the ideas of reward and punishment to recognition of moral actions. At a year old, a child is already developing a sense of justice.

Not all good

Studies with puppets are a good way of finding out what babies prefer, but we might not always like what we discover. Wyn's work with helpful and unhelpful puppets also showed that small children were happy when the puppets with which they identified (puppets who 'chose' the same food as the children) were helped, but happy when puppets unlike them (puppets who chose food the children disliked) were not helped. Wyn concluded ominously: 'This reaction seems to suggest the roots of the adult impulses toward xenophobia, prejudice and war.'

DARWIN'S BABY

It's not easy being the child of a professional biologist. Charles Darwin made detailed observations of and notes on the development of his son, William. Darwin recorded the moment at which the two-year-old boy began to deceive his parents by secretly taking food he wasn't allowed (he tried to hide the stains on his clothes). The child clearly felt guilt and shame – he had done something he was not allowed to do – but he had not suffered any punishment, so fear of discovery was not connected with fear of external consequences.

CHAPTER 8

Wasting your time in a daydream?

Do you stare out of the window, fantasizing? Is it a waste of time? What if daydreaming is good for you?

If you listened to your teachers at school, you'd get the idea that daydreaming is definitely a waste of time. In fact, the opposite could be true. Daydreaming may be the wellspring of creativity.

Bad or good?

In the 19th and early 20th centuries, professional opinion generally held that daydreaming was a problematic activity. Early psychology textbooks warned that excessive daydreaming could push people towards insanity.

An American army recruitment questionnaire circulated in World War I aimed to root out neurotic would-be soldiers by rejecting those who agreed with the statement 'I daydream frequently'. Children who daydream today might find themselves in a 'special needs' class.

Yet current estimates put the amount of time we spend daydreaming at 15–50 per cent of our waking hours so, by this token, there must be a lot of neurotic people in need of medication.

Sigmund Freud saw daydreams, like night-time dreaming, as the mind's way of revealing repressed thoughts, desires and memories. He also saw them as a kind of wish-fulfilment, in which we can have anything we want.

> '*The mind is inherently restless. It's always looking to attend to the most interesting thing in its environment. Oftentimes, the most interesting thing is going on in the internal environment.*'
>
> Jonathan Schooler,
> University of California,
> Santa Barbara

There is an increasing amount of evidence that daydreaming is constructive and useful. In the 1980s, psychologist Eric Klinger found that for people employed in dull, repetitive jobs that don't occupy the mind or in jobs that involve long periods of inactivity (such as lifeguarding), daydreaming is a way of staving off boredom and frustration and keeping the brain active. Of the group of people he studied, 75 per cent said they daydreamed to alleviate boredom.

Klinger gave participants a beeper and told them to write about any daydreams they were having each time that it sounded. He discovered that daydreaming frequency varied hugely, with people recording anything from six to 176 daydreams during a day. He found that most of our daydreaming is not ornate fantasy. Instead, it mainly consists of the rehearsal and replaying of episodes in everyday life. Counter to Freud's suggestion that daydreaming takes us to places we don't feel allowed to go in normal life, only 5 per cent of Klinger's sample reported daydreams with sexual content, and few had violent daydreams.

Better things to do?

Daydreaming is considered a problem when it prevents someone getting on with the task in hand – for example, when a schoolchild stares out of the window thinking through strategies for a computer game instead of listening to the teacher. But there is evidence that those who daydream a lot are more creative and more empathetic than those who don't. Klinger found that among a group of Israeli students, those who daydreamed were more empathetic than those who didn't.

In a study conducted by Jonathan Schooler in Santa Barbara, California, students who daydreamed while trying to read a story came up with more creative answers when asked later to think up alternative uses for everyday objects such as a coat-hanger and a toothpick than those who didn't daydream. Schooler points out that daydreaming doesn't serve the goal in hand, but it can serve longer-term goals.

So we are faced with a developmental conundrum: teachers want to stop students daydreaming because they need them to focus on the short-term goal of learning the lesson in front of them. But evidence suggests that daydreaming can make children happier and more creative in the long run.

Default mode network

Marcus E. Raichle, at the University of Washington, has used an enhanced scanning technique called functional MRI (fMRI) to discover which bits of the brain are active when we daydream. He found that parts dealing with sensory input (sights, sounds, smells) and in building and processing memory are all involved. He dubbed this set of brain functions the 'default network' because it's the activity the brain defaults to when not doing anything else. Raichle described it as the 'backbone of consciousness'.

> 'You can engage in trial action without any consequences. You can imagine yourself ridiculing your teachers or beating up your boss without actually doing it.'
>
> Psychologist
> Jerome Singer, 1966

It's been suggested that monitoring the activity of the default network might be useful in medicine; for example, in diagnosing Alzheimer's disease and assessing the effectiveness of treatments, or testing the level of consciousness in coma patients. The brain-dead have no activity in the default network, but those in a deep coma or permanent vegetative state still show 65 per cent of normal activity. Those in a state of minimal consciousness show 90 per cent of normal activity. It's possible

HARVEST YOUR DAYDREAMS

If you're not going to pay attention to what you should be doing, you might as well pay attention to what you actually are doing. Harvesting daydreams for ideas is a habit found among many successful and creative people. Einstein conceived the theory of relativity when daydreaming about riding a beam of light. George de Mestral came up with the idea for Velcro when picking burrs from his clothes and his dog's fur after a mountain walk. Many creative people carry a notebook and jot down ideas that come to them, knowing that they will otherwise forget them.

that measuring activity in the default network might be a way of anticipating which of your unconscious patients have the best chance of recovery.

Three varieties

Psychologist Jerome Singer has spent six decades researching daydreams. He had a vibrant inner life as a child and took a professional interest in daydreams as an adult, wanting to discover how different people daydream and what purpose daydreaming serves.

Singer identified three distinct types of daydreaming:

- **positive constructive daydreaming** engages in playful, vivid and wishful imagery. This is the type that is good for nurturing creativity.
- **guilty-dysphoric daydreaming** involves anxiety or dread and can be distressing; it can involve images of heroism, failure, aggression and ambition. It includes the obsessive reliving of past trauma associated with post-traumatic stress disorder (PTSD).
- **poor attentional control** is the distracted type of daydreaming, often characterized by anxiety, that plagues us when we try – and fail – to concentrate. It's the 'noonday demon' of old (see Chapter 11).

Daydreaming is good for you

Focusing on 'positive constructive daydreaming', Singer and, later, Schooler found that daydreaming can serve several broad functions:

- It helps with planning, enabling us to envisage and map out future actions. Daydreaming allows us to rehearse future events by visualizing alternative outcomes.

- It helps with problem-solving and allows creativity to flourish.
- It helps us with 'attentional cycling', allowing us to switch between focuses of attention or streams of information so that we build a more meaningful and integrated approach towards personal or external goals.
- It provides 'dishabituation' – by breaking up a task or focus we achieve more distributed practice, and that's been found to make for more solid learning. (It's why four half-hour slots of revision before a test are more effective than one unbroken two-hour stint.)

Daydreaming seems to have considerable personal and emotional benefits, helping us to develop compassion, moral reasoning, understanding of the perspectives and emotions of others, and gathering meaning from events and experiences.

WHAT DO YOU THINK OF WHEN YOU THINK OF NOTHING?

Most of us daydream. But people with Asperger's syndrome or autism tend to daydream much less than others. Russell Hurlburt at the University of Nevada studied the 'idle brain' activity of three men with Asperger's and found that they either could not grasp the concept of 'inner life' or reported only images and objects – they did not construct inner narratives.

Letting off steam

Daydreaming can also provide a safety valve. If we imagine ourselves responding aggressively to a given situation, daydreaming can relieve our tension and frustration, leaving us content to give a more measured response. Only occasionally, for some individuals, imagined aggression translates into real violence. Fantasizing about outcomes or responses can provide some satisfaction or amelioration of bad feelings if things have gone badly for us. Imagining shouting at your boss or punching your neighbour can make you feel better without you actually having to do it.

Good for whom?

Positive, constructive daydreaming is, on balance, good for personal development and satisfaction, but sometimes it might be costly in terms of external goals. That means it's good for your inner self, but not necessarily good for your public self – the 'you' that tutors and employers are relating to. Ultimately, that means you might need to moderate your level of daydreaming, since you still need to get an education or hold down a job.

EINSTEIN AND 'COMBINATORY PLAY'

Many of Einstein's ideas came to him during violin practice, and he believed that the best insights were the product of 'combinatory play' – the merging of different disciplines. Many people have defined creativity or inspiration as joining ideas or knowledge from different realms in new or unexpected ways. The most creative people are often those who can forge links or see connections between disparate concepts. Not only do the links spring up during daydreaming, but the raw material is often garnered during apparently unrelated activities such as playing the violin and thinking of equations.

Day-nightmares

The bad type of daydreaming is, in extremes, associated with mental distress and psychological illness. The nightmare daydreaming of depression is rumination – the constant picking over of distressing memories or thoughts. Instead of the mind drifting to pleasurable plans for a hot date or useful inventions, it returns repeatedly to the replaying of past mistakes or slights. Like picking at a scab, it doesn't make the wound any better, but prolongs the agony. A common feature of PTSD is replaying the traumatic incident, either consciously or in flashbacks. Again, it's not a healthy type of daydreaming. In depressed people, a particular part of the default network becomes very active. The subgenual anterior cingulate cortex, more helpfully known as the 'sadness node', goes into overdrive as people suffering from depression ruminate or relive painful memories.

> '**What is most truly human about man, what is perhaps his greatest gift derived from evolution and perhaps his greatest resource in his mastery of the environment and of himself, is his capacity for fantasy.**'
>
> Psychologist
> Jerome Singer

CHAPTER 9

Would you do that again?

What triggers responses in us?
Conditioning can forge strange
links between stimuli and actions.

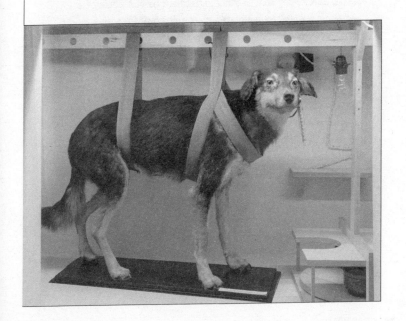

Do you get hungry if you look at pictures in a food magazine? Do you feel uncomfortable if you see a video about surgery? Your brain makes connections between the knowledge you have received and specific bodily functions and sensations. Responding to some stimuli is instinctive – salivating when we see food, for example. Other responses are conditioned – if we have had bad experiences at the dentist, our anxiety levels might rise as soon as we walk through the surgery door.

PAVLOV'S DOGS

Russian physiologist Ivan Pavlov (1849–1936) studied the workings of the digestive system. While conducting experiments with dogs, he discovered the conditioned reflex – a learned physical response to a stimulus. Dogs will usually salivate whenever they see food; it is an instinct that prepares the dog to eat. The food is a primary stimulus that produces a response – salivating. Pavlov repeatedly made a noise with a buzzer, whistle, bell, tuning fork or other instrument before feeding his experimental dogs. As usual, the dogs salivated when their food arrived. After a while, the dogs began to associate the noise Pavlov made with the imminent arrival of food and began salivating as soon as they heard it – before they even saw the food. Although salivating is an automatic response that can't be controlled directly, the dogs' brains had set up a connection between the sound and the arrival of food, so this secondary stimulus produced the same response.

Conditioned responses can make us fear things that are not, in themselves, scary. Conditioning can also lead us to do things or not do them because of the response they elicit. This type of conditioning is used in child rearing and dog training.

A job frightening small children

Whatever you think of experimenting on animals, as Pavlov did, few people would now condone the notorious 'Little Albert' experiments.

In 1919, psychologists John B. Watson (see Chapter 6) and Rosalie Rayner used a nine-month-old baby boy in their behaviour experiments. He was known as 'Little Albert', although in 2009 his real name was revealed to be Douglas Merritte. Watson and Rayner began the experiment by exposing 'Little Albert' to a range of objects and animals, including a white laboratory rat. He was not afraid of any of them. Then Watson and Rayner proceeded to frighten 'Albert'. When he touched the rat, they made a loud noise behind him by

THE LAW OF EFFECT

Soon after the publication of Pavlov's experiments on classical conditioning in dogs in Russia, Edward Thorndike began working on operant conditioning with cats in the USA. He built a 'puzzle box' that a cat could only escape from by pressing a lever or pulling on a loop. He put a hungry cat in the box. It had to free itself before it could get any food. Thorndike noted that it took quite a while for the cat to stumble on the escape mechanism the first time, but with successive box-trips it took the cat less and less time to escape. Thorndike defined the law of effect: a pleasing after-effect strengthens (encourages) the action that produced it. Modern psychologists would call this 'positive reinforcement' – the good effect of escaping the box reinforces the cat's action of using the lever or loop.

striking a piece of metal with a hammer. The boy cried. They did this repeatedly until Albert cried whenever he saw the rat. As soon as it appeared, Albert would turn away and try to escape.

The association extended to other furry objects, so that Albert also became afraid of a rabbit, a dog, a furry coat and Watson himself, when he appeared in a Santa Claus mask with a fuzzy beard (which sounds as though it might have been frightening even without the conditioning). The study showed that the kind of classical conditioning Pavlov had managed with dogs was also applicable to humans.

CLASSICAL AND OPERANT CONDITIONING

Classical conditioning is the same as Pavlovian conditioning: the body is taught by repeated exposure to give a response to an unrelated stimulus, such as drooling at the sound of a bell because the bell is known to signal food.

Operant conditioning is strengthening or weakening a spontaneous action by means of rewarding or punishing it.

For example, if a rat finds that pressing a lever delivers a drink of sugar water, it will perform the action repeatedly. If pressing the lever delivers an electric shock, the rat will stop pressing it. The positive and negative consequences reinforce the rat's behaviour.

Not so good

A great deal was wrong with Watson and Rayner's experiment, not least that it was unethical and cruel. Little Albert was not desensitized afterwards, so presumably remained afraid of rats, rabbits and other furry animals. He moved away with his parents and there was no opportunity for follow-up studies or therapy. In fact, he died at the age of six from hydrocephalus, which he'd had since birth. Contrary to Watson's claims that he was a normal, healthy baby, Albert was not healthy (and

Watson probably knew this). The child was therefore unsuitable as a subject representing normal development. Furthermore, Watson and Rayner had no system for measuring Albert's responses other than their own subjective judgements.

Better conditions

In 1924, Mary Cover Jones used conditioning more ethically to help a child with a phobia of white, furry things. The child, Peter, was terrified of a white rabbit. Over time, the experimenter brought Peter and the rabbit closer together until eventually the boy was able to pet and play with the rabbit without fear. Other children, who were not afraid of the rabbit, were present in the room, modelling normal responses to the animal.

Making things better

The Peter experiment was an early foray into behavioural therapy, which aims to retrain a person's thinking and behaviour. Several types of conditioning are used in therapy, teaching and other kinds of behaviour modification. They can involve punishment or reward.

A punishment is a negative reinforcement – each time the subject does something, a bad thing happens. It aims to reduce an unwanted behaviour. A reward is a positive reinforcement that aims to increase a desired behaviour – giving children a sticker for picking up toys they have dropped, for instance.

Most studies suggest that positive reinforcement is more effective than negative reinforcement (see Chapter 16).

We do it all the time

We use elements of conditioning, and positive and negative reinforcement all the time without really thinking. When childcare manuals suggest giving a child a bedtime routine, they are utilizing a form of conditioning.

STAGES OF LOSING FEAR OF RABBITS

Mary Cover Jones reported the following stages of interaction between Peter and the rabbit:

   A. Rabbit anywhere in the room in a cage causes fear reactions.
   B. Rabbit 12 feet away in cage tolerated.
   C. Rabbit 4 feet away in cage tolerated.
   D. Rabbit 3 feet away in cage tolerated.
   E. Rabbit close in cage tolerated.
   F. Rabbit free in room tolerated.
   G. Rabbit touched when experimenter holds it.
   H. Rabbit touched when free in room.
   I. Rabbit defied by spitting at it, throwing things at it, imitating it.
   J. Rabbit allowed on tray of high chair.
   K. Squats in defenceless position beside rabbit.
   L. Helps experimenter to carry rabbit to its cage.
   M. Holds rabbit on lap.
   N. Stays alone in room with rabbit.
   O. Allows rabbit in playpen with him.
   P. Fondles rabbit affectionately.
   Q. Lets rabbit nibble his fingers.

The child who every day has a warm bath, a story and then goes to sleep will, after a while, start to feel sleepy because the warm bath and story always lead to sleep. A dog that is taken for a walk when a child comes home from school will get excited on hearing the door open in the afternoon.

5:1

Studies have found that in trying to adjust the behaviour of children, a ratio of 5:1 (praise: criticism) is most effective. According to other studies, the same ratio of praise and criticism works in keeping marriages stable.

CHAPTER 10

Why won't you get up?

Why do teenagers stay in bed half the day? Are they just lazy?

Anyone who lives with a teenager, or who remembers being one, will know that teens like to stay in bed until well past normal getting-up time. They also like to stay up until well beyond any normal going-to-bed time. Left to their own devices, they'll often stay up until 4am and sleep until the afternoon.

Is it just perversity and rebellion? Or is there a good reason for such antisocial timekeeping?

Your personal clock

Everyone has an internal (or body) clock that regulates the natural cycles of the body. This pattern of daily activities in your body is called the 'circadian rhythm' and it determines such things as when you are most active, when you feel tired, and so on. Most of us are not able to work entirely in synch with our circadian rhythms as we are bound by convention and financial need to go to work at hours of our employers' choosing, to get our children up and off to school, to feed hungry babies or be awake for deliveries and appointments.

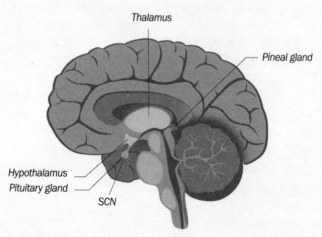

The body clock is located in the hypothalamic suprachiasmatic nucleus (SCN), a tiny group of cells at the base of the brain.

Night owls and larks

We're used to the idea that some people are most alert and amenable to work in the evenings and others function best in the mornings. This distinction between 'evening people' and 'morning people' is commonly acknowledged with the labels 'night owls' and 'larks'. If you like to stay up late and get up late, you're a night owl. If you like to go to bed early and get up early, you're a lark. There's nothing wrong with either, but if you're a lark you'll struggle with working late into the evening, and if you're a night owl you'll find it challenging to do a job that involves a commute starting at 6am.

HOW YOU'RE LIKE A MUSHROOM

Humans are not the only entities to have circadian rhythms. Many – perhaps all – organisms on Earth have body clocks that are attuned approximately to a 24-hour day. Nocturnal animals sleep all day and hunt at night, but they still work to a 24-hour cycle. Even fungi have circadian rhythms and produce spores at a particular time of day. Scientists researching circadian rhythms often work with a fungus called *Neurospora crassa*. They have found genes which control the relation of activity in the fungus to times of day. Mutations in these genes interfere with the fungus's body clock. Are teenagers and mushrooms related after all?

Night owls and larks are at opposite ends of the normal spectrum for circadian rhythms. Night owls might need a loud alarm to get them up in the morning, but they will get up. They are not generally dysfunctional.

> *'There's a biological predisposition for going to bed late and getting up late. Clearly you can impose upon that even worse habits, but they are not lazy.'*
>
> Russell Foster, Professor of Circadian Neuroscience, Oxford University

Jet lag

Whether you're a night owl or a lark, if you've taken a long flight that crosses several time zones, you are likely to have experienced jet lag. It occurs when your circadian rhythms have been severely disrupted – for example, by being expected to sleep when your body thinks it's the middle of the day, or to attend meetings when your body thinks it's after midnight.

Over a few days, exposure to your current pattern of night and day nudges your body clock into synch with the local time zone and you feel better.

The teenage body clock

Mary Carskadon, Professor of Human Behaviour at Brown University, USA, has carried out extensive research into the circadian rhythms of children and adolescents. Her findings bear out what any teenager will tell you – they really *can't* get up at 7am and function normally.

At puberty, the brain undergoes many changes, including changes to the biological body clock. This equips adolescents for teenage life, enabling them to stay up late at parties and gigs and to sleep through any number of alarm clocks and shouting parents until midday or later. Unfortunately, as Carskadon

CAN YOU AVOID JET LAG?

The chemical melatonin is a hormone produced in the pineal gland, deep in the brain. It plays an important role in regulating circadian rhythms. Melatonin is produced when it gets dark, and helps to regulate the body's temperature during sleep. Trials have found that taking melatonin by mouth at bedtime after a flight reduces jet lag in nine out of ten people. Jet lag is worst, and melatonin most effective, when flying east and crossing four or more time zones.

Combining sleeping tablets to get to sleep and coffee to stay awake is not an effective treatment for jet lag. Sleeping on the plane doesn't reduce jet lag unless it's at a time when you would normally sleep. Neither of these approaches readjusts the body's internal clock. Dehydration makes jet lag worse, so drinking alcohol to while away the hours won't work.

If you're only travelling for a couple of days, it's not worth trying to reset your body clock on the trip. Otherwise, stay in the dark for at least three hours after arriving if you're flying east. If you're flying west, get out into daylight when you arrive.

points out, it doesn't equip them for a school or college day that starts at 8–8.30am.

Carskadon has shown that even if teenagers go to bed early, they don't get to sleep then. Getting up early for school means they are sleep-deprived during the week and desperate to catch up with sleep at the weekend – hence staying in bed until the afternoon. Teens need 9¼ hours' sleep, and generally can't get to sleep before 11pm – it's simply not possible to have the sleep they need and get to school on time. Carskadon's studies show that the mismatch between the school day and the biological needs of adolescents has many effects, including poor performance at studies and under-achievement. Carskadon believes that the school day should be changed to accommodate the different biological rhythms of teens, but the disruption it would cause for everyone else means it is unlikely to happen.

Sleeping sickness?

Too little sleep can also lead to psychiatric disorders, including depression. Psychologist Jane Ansell found that around 50 per cent of teenagers in Scotland are sleep-deprived. Some have been misdiagnosed with attention deficit hyperactivity disorder (ADHD) and other psychological problems, when all they need is more sleep.

ALT-SHIFT-DELETE?

With shift workers, the body clock gets messed around endlessly and this has serious health implications. A study published in 2014 found that working a night-shift disrupted the activity of nearly 6 per cent of our genes. As the genes are not evenly disturbed, different parts of the body end up working to different clocks. One of the researchers likened it to having clocks in each room in a house that are set to different times. The lasting effects could include physical as well as psychological harm, such as obesity, diabetes and heart disease.

Can you be bored to death?

Being bored has more going for it than you might imagine.

If you have children, you may be familiar with the pained cry, 'I'm bored' in the holidays. Does boredom serve a purpose? Why do we get bored?

This boring cave . . .

In prehistory, did cave men (and cave women) get bored? Is that why they painted on the walls? If so, it was the women who were most bored, as research into comparative finger and palm sizes shows that most cave paintings were created by women. And when they had had enough of painting recognizable things, they seem to have played a game that involved jumping as high as they could, as shown by groups of circles made with fingertips on the roofs of some caves.

> *'Boredom is not an end product; it is, comparatively, rather an early stage in life and art. You've got to go by or past or through boredom, as through a filter, before the clear product emerges.'*
>
> F. Scott Fitzgerald

The noonday demon

Boredom with doing a routine task is not the same as boredom with not doing anything. Many people have genuinely boring jobs – they take objects off shelves and put them into trolleys to fulfil orders in a warehouse or supermarket. They clean the floors of empty buildings. They do repetitive tasks that are unfulfilling and don't involve engaging with other people.

Other people have jobs that should be less boring, but still they can't settle to them. We stare at the computer screen, or out of the window, fiddle with our phones, flick to a social network site, even if our work is something that interests us in principle. It's not a new problem. This mind-wandering was known to medieval monks as 'acedia' ('άκηδία') and called the noonday demon (a name since appropriated for depression). It was familiar to the Desert Fathers, those early Christian ascetics who spent their time in contemplation, philosophizing and study. This is not boredom of the same kind. It's being amenable to distractions even though we have something to do that should be challenging and engaging.

These early writers recognized the problem of trying to stay focused on intellectual activity in solitude. St Cassian writes of Paul – living in the desert but provided with all he needs, spending his days making things from date palms and then, at the end of the year, burning them all because: 'without working with his hands a monk cannot endure to abide in his place, nor can he climb any nearer the summit of holiness: and though necessity of making a livelihood in no way demands it, let it be done for the sole purging of the heart, the steadying of thought, perseverance in the cell, and the conquest and final overthrow of accidie itself.'

This recalls the adage 'the devil makes work for idle hands'. The monk who has nothing he needs to do, must yet do something, as to do nothing is dangerous. Intellectual work makes him especially prone to this type of mind-wandering or ennui. So the monk must work with his hands if he is to be able to tolerate the work of thinking.

'The demon of acedia – also called the noonday demon – is the one that causes the most serious trouble of all. He presses his attack upon the monk about the fourth hour and besieges the soul until the eighth hour. First of all he makes it seem that the sun barely moves, if at all, and that the day is fifty hours long. Then he constrains the monk to look constantly out the windows, to walk outside the cell, to gaze carefully at the sun to determine how far it stands from the ninth hour, to look now this way and now that to see if perhaps [one of the brethren appears from his cell]. . . . This demon drives him along to desire other sites where he can more easily procure life's necessities, more readily find work and make a real success of himself.'

Evagrius the Solitary, AD345–399

Hands and brains

Modern neuroscience suggests another possibility, more practical than demons with a brief to distract the holy. A study on rats reveals that lack of physical activity actually changes the shape of brain cells.

Researchers at Wayne State University School of Medicine, in Detroit, Michigan, divided twelve rats into two groups. One group was put into cages with a running wheel and the rats were soon running five kilometres a day. The other group was put into cages with no wheels, so the rats had a sedentary lifestyle. After three months, the inactive rats had grown extra branches on the neurons in part of their brains. This made them extra-sensitive to stimuli and prone to send extra nerve signals around the brain. The researchers were interested in the implications for heart disease. However, it seems that a 'jumpy brain' from inactivity might be a genuine neurological phenomenon rather than simply a predisposition to distraction.

> *My soul is impatient with itself, as with a bothersome child; its restlessness keeps growing and is forever the same. Everything interests me, but nothing holds me. I attend to everything, dreaming all the while.'*
>
> Fernando Pessoa, 1888–1935, poet and writer

Sick of doing nothing

Being bored because you have nothing to do is rather different from failure to engage fully or pay attention to the task in hand. It's possible to be bored because there is too much choice of activity. For example, the child bored in the holidays might have many options – riding a bike, playing with toys or friends, reading – but none of them appeals. This, like being bored while doing a task, is a failure of attention. None of the possible activities holds the child's attention.

We commonly think of boredom as something rather trivial, but it has been associated with depression and anxiety

'She only said, "My life is dreary"': W. E. F. Britten's sketch of Tennyson's bored heroine, Mariana.

disorders. The phrase 'bored to death' was coined by Charles Dickens in *Bleak House*. It was the first instance in which the word 'bored' was used to mean a kind of spiritual malady. The wealthy, sombre Lady Dedlock is described as being 'in the desolation of Boredom and the clutch of the Giant Despair'.

Boredom – having nothing to do – has also been blamed for criminal and antisocial behaviour and implicated in risky behaviours such as drug-taking and compulsive gambling, with people seeking thrills to enliven their uneventful lives.

The distress boredom causes is acknowledged in its use as a punishment in prisons the world over. It's important, though, to get the balance right. Boredom is a matter of life and death in more ways than one. If prisoners are bored, it can be fatal. When asked why he had killed another inmate at Long Larton prison in England, a prisoner said, 'I'm bored, it was something to do.' It's an excuse echoed by many a 'bored' teenager.

The 17th-century philosopher and mathematician Blaise Pascal thought boredom more than trivial. He saw it as a kind of terrible existential angst which could only be dealt with by filling life with purpose, and that purpose was God. Writing in *Pensées*, Pascal said: 'We seek rest in a struggle against some obstacles. And when we have overcome these, rest proves unbearable because of the boredom it produces . . . only an infinite and immutable object – that is, God himself – can fill this infinite abyss.'

> *'And I am bored to death with it. Bored to death with this place, bored to death with my life, bored to death with myself.'*
>
> Lady Dedlock, *Bleak House*, Charles Dickens, 1852–3

Later, both Arthur Schopenhauer (1788–1860) and Martin Heidegger (1889–1976) picked up this theme, with a predictably gloomy outcome. Schopenhauer maintained that if life had any real value we would never be bored, because life itself would suffice. Heidegger concurred, though with not quite so damning a verdict on life: 'Profound boredom, drifting here and there in the abysses of our existence like a muffling fog, removes all things and men and oneself along with it into a remarkable indifference. This boredom reveals being as a whole.'

So – what should you do with that bored child?

First, let the child be bored for a bit. Being bored is useful; boredom is the mother of many a creative project (see the F. Scott Fitzgerald quote on page 90). Children need to learn to occupy

Charles Dickens' anguished Lady Dedlock – the first fictional character to be 'bored to death'.

themselves and to manage their time – it's a vital life-skill. They need to work out what interests them and what doesn't; they can't do that if they are fed a constant stream of amusements.

The only thing psychologists think you shouldn't do is leave your bored children in front of a TV or computer screen or playing with a mobile phone. Screen-based activities produce little doses of dopamine in the brain, a chemical that contributes to learning and concentration. It's easy for children to become accustomed to the higher level of dopamine, and then find it harder to concentrate on activities that don't deliver the dopamine hit. Children who use screens too much of the time can find it harder to concentrate when doing non-screen activities. If you want to wean them off screen-time later, you'll have a harder job on your hands than helping them find something to do now.

Of course, the same goes for you. If you're bored, a computer game, social networking session or a box-set of DVDs may keep you happy and entertained, but can make you more prone to being bored later on.

SCREENS OR SCREAMS?

It's tempting for weary parents to park a toddler in front of a TV screen or give them a table computer or mobile phone to play with, but the American Academy of Pediatrics recommends against it. Their recommended screen-times for children are:

- Up to 2 years old: none
- Ages 3–6 years old: 4–6 hours per week, with the activities discussed and chosen carefully
- Ages 6–14: 6–8 hours a week (a 2010 survey found that young people aged 8–18 spend an average of 7½ hours a day on electronic media)
- Ages 14–18: let them set their own limits, in discussion with you. They need to learn to be self-regulating.

CHAPTER 12

How cruel can you be?

You might think you would never harm someone who hasn't harmed you. But are you sure?

Would you deliver electric shocks to another person who was innocent of any crime, just because someone told you to? We are far more susceptible to authority than we might like to think.

The incredulity with which Ron Jones' students met his account of Nazi Germany is a common response (see Chapter 3). Most normal people find it hard to believe that ordinary German citizens, just like any one of us, could be persuaded to torture and execute their fellow humans. Were the Germans who became Nazis somehow different from the rest of us?

'Where they burn books, they will, in the end, burn human beings too.' Writing in the 19th century, the poet and playwright Heinrich Heine foresaw the terrible consequences of intolerance combined with 'group think'.

The Milgram experiment

Stanley Milgram, a psychologist at Yale University, Connecticut, was interested in the excuse given by many ex-Nazis that they had just been following orders. He was curious to discover how far ordinary people would go to ingratiate themselves with their superiors. So he decided to find out.

In 1961, Milgram recruited 40 volunteers to help with a study of learning; all of them were men between the ages of 20 and 50 (and thus comparable to those who might have become SS guards in Nazi Germany). He told them that they would be randomly allocated roles as learners or teachers, but in fact all volunteers were to be teachers and all the 'learners' were confederates of Milgram's – actors briefed to play their part. The teachers were instructed to ask questions of a learner in an adjacent room. They were told the learner would be strapped to a chair with two electrodes attached to his body. If the learner got a question wrong, the volunteer (the teacher) would administer an electric shock. The volunteer was told that shocks would be painful but not harmful. The shocks would be mild to start with, but become more extreme as the learner gave more wrong answers, increasing progressively (the volunteers were told) from 15 volts to 450 volts – a dangerous level of shock.

> '*When you think of the long and gloomy history of man, you will find more hideous crimes have been committed in the name of obedience than have ever been committed in the name of rebellion.*'
>
> C. P. Snow, 1961

Scripted torture

As the experiment progressed, the learner could be heard screaming, struggling in their chair and begging to be released as they were apparently subjected to more and more pain. At 300 volts, following a script, the learner banged on the wall, begging to be let out. Above that level of shock, the learner remained silent. The volunteer was told to consider silence to be a wrong answer and continue increasing the shocks. The experimenter sat in the room with the volunteer and, if the volunteer baulked at the idea of administering a shock, encouraged him by using the following scripted prompts, in order:

1. Please continue.
2. The experiment requires you to continue.
3. It is absolutely essential that you continue.
4. You have no other choice but to continue.

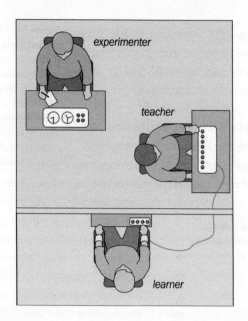

experimenter

teacher

learner

Just say yes

The results that Milgram reported were alarming. All the volunteers continued to administer shocks up to 300 volts and nearly two-thirds (65 per cent) of volunteers continued all the way to the highest level of shock, 450 volts. Milgram concluded that we have an overwhelming urge to obey an authority figure – even one as seemingly powerless as a scientific researcher.

Milgram debriefed his volunteers, explaining the experiment to them and noted down how they reacted. He identified three types of volunteer by their responses:

- Obeyed, but justified themselves – they shifted responsibility on to the experimenter or, in some cases, the learner (for their stupidity).
- Obeyed, but blamed themselves – they felt bad about what they had done. Milgram felt this group might act differently if they found themselves in a similar situation in future.

- Rebelled – refused to continue with the experiment, citing the primacy of the learner's wellbeing over the needs of the experiment.

> '*Could it be that Eichmann and his million accomplices in the Holocaust were just following orders? Could we call them all accomplices?'*
>
> Stanley Milgram, 1974

The circumstances of obedience

Milgram repeated his experiment, varying some aspects of the setting to see which factors affected levels of obedience. He found that obedience levels were higher in the hallowed environment of Yale University, but lower in a run-down office in the city. Levels were higher when the experimenter wore a lab coat and lower when he wore ordinary clothes. People were more obedient when the authority figure (the experimenter) was in the room rather than giving instructions by telephone. Finally, obedience rose considerably when people did not have to press the switch themselves to administer the shock, but delegated the task to an assistant.

> '*I set up a simple experiment at Yale University to test how much pain an ordinary citizen would inflict on another person simply because he was ordered to by an experimental scientist. Stark authority was pitted against the subjects' [participants'] strongest moral imperatives against hurting others, and, with the subjects' [participants'] ears ringing with the screams of the victims, authority won more often than not. The extreme willingness of adults to go to almost any lengths on the command of an authority constitutes the chief finding of the study and the fact most urgently demanding explanation.'*
>
> Stanley Milgram, 1974

Milgram's agency theory

To account for the alacrity with which ordinary people would behave in appalling ways, Milgram proposed his 'agency theory'. He suggested that we have two different states: autonomous and 'agentic'.

In an autonomous state, people make their own choices and take responsibility for their actions. They are governed by their own sets of values and standards. In the agentic state, they act as agents, carrying out orders and feeling they bear no responsibility for their actions as they have not personally sanctioned them.

When faced with a figure of authority, Milgram claimed, most people underwent an 'agentic shift' from the autonomous to the obedient state. This explains why US soldiers obeyed orders to kill unarmed Vietnamese civilians in the village of My Lai in 1968, why Serbian soldiers in Bosnia raped women as an act of war, and why many atrocities have been committed against the innocent in Rwanda, the Baltic States and Iraq over the past 20 years. Critics complain that no mechanism for this shift has been demonstrated and it's hard to see how it could be measured.

> 'Ordinary people, simply doing their jobs, and without any particular hostility on their part, can become agents in a terrible destructive process. Moreover, even when the destructive effects of their work become patently clear, and they are asked to carry out actions incompatible with fundamental standards of morality, relatively few people have the resources needed to resist authority.'
>
> Stanley Milgram, 1974

Traumatized survivors of the My Lai massacre.

Was it true?

Milgram's methodology has been criticized, as has his practice of leading the volunteers to believe they were harming someone. In 2013, psychologist Gina Perry published the findings of her research into the Milgram archive. Milgram's presentation of his results had been somewhat selective, as he had conflated all the studies to give a 65 per cent obedience rating. Some volunteers had suspected the deception, while others had surreptitiously 'inflicted' shocks of a lower voltage (although the intensity of the screams still increased). Some had asked to check up on the learner or to swap places with him (requests that had been refused), and the experimenter had frequently strayed from the script to bully or coerce the volunteer into complying. Furthermore, Milgram's sample was a self-selected group of American males. Can this be considered representative of people in general?

Whether or not the results of Milgram's study are reliable or statistically accurate, it's clear that a significant proportion of people will take obedience far enough to willingly inflict serious harm on others. Perhaps there isn't an inner Nazi in all of us, but there is an alarming tendency to do as we are told, even if we doubt the morality or wisdom of the order.

The Nazis exploited human psychological weaknesses – the need for group acceptance and a fear of reprisals – with devastating results.

FROM THE HORSE'S MOUTH

At his trial in Jerusalem in 1960, Nazi war criminal Adolf Eichmann referred repeatedly to his role as one of impotent obedience, even though he had been largely in charge of organizing the Holocaust. He described himself as 'one of the many horses pulling the wagon and [I] couldn't escape left or right because of the will of the driver'.

'From my childhood, obedience was something I could not get out of my system. When I entered the armed services at the age of 27, I found being obedient not a bit more difficult than it had been during my life to that point. It was unthinkable that I would not follow orders.

'I personally had nothing to do with this. My job was to observe and report on it.

'Obeying an order was the most important thing to me. It could be that is in the nature of the German.

'Now that I look back, I realize that a life predicated on being obedient and taking orders is a very comfortable life indeed. Living in such a way reduces to a minimum one's own need to think.'

Adolf Eichmann, 1960

CHAPTER 13

Why are you wasting my time?

It is rude to waste someone's time. So you have to persuade them that it hasn't been wasted.

We know that time is a valuable commodity and we get frustrated when we are forced to waste it. Never mind that most of us waste a lot of time anyway – it's different if you've chosen to watch junk TV or stare out of the window. What we really don't like is being *forced* to wait.

Queue quietly

Unlikely as it may seem, there are people who specialize in queue management – they make people behave well in queues and encourage them to feel they are having as good an experience as possible. If people in a queue feel ignored, they are more likely to be grouchy, cause trouble, or spend less money, or choose not to return. Investing in queue management can pay dividends.

THE TOO-EFFICIENT AIRPORT

Houston airport in the USA was receiving a large number of complaints from passengers about the length of time they had to wait to reclaim their baggage. The airport responded by employing more luggage handlers so that bags could be delivered more quickly. The average wait was cut to eight minutes – but the level of complaints remained the same.

The airport's next solution was a stroke of genius. They moved the baggage reclaim area much further away from the arrival gates. The passengers had to walk a lot further than before, so they used up most of their waiting time walking to the carousels. Instead of waiting for eight minutes at the carousel, they walked for six and waited for two.

Complaints stopped. People no longer felt that they were wasting their time.

Organizations selling services that involve a lot of waiting or queuing take advantage of psychological research into queuing and waiting behaviour. If customers can be persuaded to be happy about the queue, they are much less likely to complain about their treatment and far more likely to return. Walt Disney employs 75 industrial engineers around the world to help with queue management in its theme parks.

How long do I have to wait?

People typically overestimate the length of time they have been waiting. If asked, they claim to have waited, on average, 36 per cent longer than they really have been waiting.

Queue rage is a phenomenon every bit as real as road rage, but it can be reduced if people in the queue are kept informed. If they know how long they will have to wait, they are less likely to get angry, unless the wait is longer than they were led to expect. Some theme parks advertise slightly exaggerated waiting times for the rides so that people are pleasantly surprised by the length of the wait. They come away feeling they didn't have to wait too long and that they have somehow beaten the system. For example, in the ordinary course of events people might grumble about having to wait for 30 minutes. But if they expect to wait 40 minutes they are less likely to complain because they now feel they are 'up' by ten minutes.

You aren't doing nothing

Another way of keeping people calm is to give them something to do – watching adverts or news updates on a screen, for example. Today, screens are everywhere. You can watch the news on a bus, on the train, at the post office and in hospital waiting rooms. Sometimes we might be rewarded (or bribed) with free sweets in a hotel reception area or with free coffee in a clinic or hair salon. This is scant payment for our precious time, but we don't think of it that way because the value of our time is acknowledged and we are offered something in return – regardless of the fact that it is virtually worthless.

Don't worry

One reason people don't like waiting is that it makes them anxious. They are worried about the time they are losing, and sometimes about what is coming after the wait (a session in the dentist's chair, for example). If the wait is too long, they might also worry that they have been forgotten.

Speaking to someone or being moved to a different area helps to alleviate anxiety as people feel they are being 'seen to' or 'dealt with'. Waiting as part of a process annoys people less than waiting for a process to begin. So although it makes no difference to the length of your waiting time at the doctor's surgery, if you are moved from one waiting area to another after 15 minutes it feels less frustrating.

If a nurse takes a quick history of your problem, or asks you to fill in a questionnaire, you will feel even better as it seems you are no longer wasting time – even if the nurse does nothing with the information you provide.

When waiting is sold to you

Have you ever walked past an Apple store the day a new iPad or iPhone is released? The queue often goes around the block – yet no one minds. The same was true of people queuing at midnight for the latest Harry Potter novel. It's not the same as queuing for the sales or for tickets to a popular concert or festival – there's a limited supply of those and only one chance to buy. No one believes Apple won't make as many iPhones as they can sell, the iPhones just won't all be available on the first day.

> 'Often the psychology of queuing is more important than the statistics of the wait itself.'
>
> Richard Larson, Massachusetts Institute of Technology (MIT)

The illusion of exclusivity is created by a high price point – and by queuing. People will spend ages in a queue just so they can buy a new phone a couple of days ahead of other people.

They will even boast about how long they have been queuing and bond with other people in the queue.

Agency and its lack

One of the reasons we don't like to queue is that we feel we have no control over the situation. In the language of psychology, this 'lack of agency' makes us feel bad. Agency is the sense that we are acting as independent agents, that our fate is in our own hands. It is a combination of empowerment and self-determination.

Lack of agency on a large scale is very damaging, leading to frustration, anger and even depression. When asked to give an account of their personal history and circumstances, people with depression frequently locate the source of their problems outside themselves. They talk of things happening *to* them, and of what others have done that has had an impact *on* them. People who are not depressed tend to put themselves at the centre of their own narrative, saying what *they* have done, or how *they* have responded to outside events. They don't represent external events as the driving force of their lives.

Bread, circuses and talent shows

It is possible to distract people from their lack of agency, and many political systems have attempted to do this (often successfully). When people feel disempowered, they will seize on any apparently power-bestowing situation or anything that apparently validates their worth.

Today people are buffeted by economic and political forces beyond

'Already long ago, from when we sold our vote to no man, the People have abdicated our duties; for the People who once upon a time handed out military command, high civil office, legions – everything, now restrains itself and anxiously hopes for just two things: bread and circuses.'

Juvenal, *Satires* (10)

their control, and therefore feel powerless. In response, they adopt small acts of agency, or *faux*-agency, by voting on talent contests and reality shows and by 'making their voices heard' on social media. Did you vote for the talent show winner? *You* made that happen. Did you tweet your disgust at a news story? You are part of 'the conversation'.

BUTTONS THAT DO NOTHING

You know those buttons at traffic junctions that you press to change the lights? Usually they do nothing of the sort. The lights are on a fixed sequence and the buttons have no effect on them whatsoever. They are known as 'placebo buttons'. The 'Close Doors' button in a lift often works (or doesn't) on a similar principle. These buttons give us a sense of agency and make us feel less powerless while waiting for the lights to change or for the lift to arrive.

CHAPTER 14

Why didn't anybody help?

Is failing to help a person in trouble a simple act of heartlessness? Or is it more complicated than that?

Have you ever seen something bad happen, and noticed people walking past without helping? Perhaps you also walked past without helping? Sometimes we tell ourselves we don't want to get involved. If it's a domestic dispute, we can say it's none of our business. If it's a dangerous situation, we can say we don't want to get hurt. But what if someone has an accident, or collapses, or is having a fit? People will still walk past when there is no risk of danger to themselves or any chance of intruding in an unwelcome way. It's called 'bystander apathy', and it doesn't simply apply to helping others; it can even extend to protecting ourselves.

THE MURDER OF KITTY GENOVESE

Kitty Genovese was an Italian-American woman who was attacked and murdered in New York in 1964. The newspapers reported that 38 people had witnessed or heard the attack, but none of them came to Kitty's aid. Later accounts disputed that so many people had been aware of the attack or that no one had helped. But whatever the events, the case sparked a far-reaching psychological study into this 'bystander apathy' – sometimes now also referred to as 'Genovese syndrome'.

Who will help?

While it would probably be dangerous to intervene in a murder, getting help for someone experiencing an epileptic fit would seem an obvious and humane thing to do. Yet surprisingly few people will go to the victim's aid.

In 1968, prompted by the Genovese case, John Darley and Bibb Latané set up an experiment at Columbia University to discover whether people would help a stranger in distress. They asked for volunteers to take part in a psychological study about personal problems. As usual with psychology experiments, the story was a cover. Because the issues discussed were private, all the conversations were to take place over intercom systems. It was important that the participants could not see one another. There were one, four or no other participants in each study.

Part way through a discussion, one of the participants (in reality a confederate of the researchers) would fake a seizure. They stuttered, asked for help, said they were ill, became increasingly distressed and said they felt they would die. The other participants could hear this – and one another – over the intercom. They had been told at the start of the experiment that it was important for all participants to remain anonymous – rushing to someone's aid would compromise that anonymity.

Darley and Latané found that if there was a larger number of people involved in the discussion, it was less likely that any of them would help. Even though they could not see the other participants, they knew they were there. It seemed that each person felt that they had less responsibility towards the stranger in distress because there were other people around who would help. Individual background and gender made no difference to whether people helped or not.

When a participant was the only person involved, he/she sought help 85 per cent of the time. This fell to 31 per cent when several people were involved in the discussion.

Not uncaring

The people who didn't help weren't unfeeling towards the sufferer. They showed symptoms of worry and distress, including sweating and trembling. They appeared to be caught between fear of embarrassment or spoiling the experiment and distress at the fate of the person having a seizure. When there were no extra participants, the person was much more likely to act. When there were others, they clearly hoped that someone else would do what was needed: they *relied* upon someone else doing it.

HUMAN KINDNESS?

In 2011, a two-year-old girl was run down by a truck in the Chinese city of Foshan. The girl, Yue Yue, lay in the road for seven minutes, and was run over again, while people walked and cycled past her. Finally a woman moved the child to the side of the road. Yue Yue later died of her injuries in hospital. In response to the global outrage that followed, it was suggested that individuals had been reluctant to help because they didn't want to be liable for the girl's medical bills. In Guangdong province there were discussions about introducing a law to make it illegal to ignore a person in distress.

But this explaining away of the callous nature of human behaviour appears to have been a red herring. In 2009, in Richmond, California, 20 people witnessed the rape and murder of a 15-year-old girl. No one called for help, and no one intervened; some people even filmed it on their phones. Bystanders later said they thought it was a joke – people messing about – but no one had checked, and no one had asked if she needed help.

How bullies get away with it

If people avoid getting involved to stop a rape or a murder, or even to help an injured toddler, is it surprising that bullies thrive and continue to torment their targets? Whether in the workplace or the playground, many people turn a blind eye to bullying as to other types of distress. And the more witnesses there are, the more each one sees it as 'not my problem' and leaves it for someone else to sort out.

One reason for not intervening is what psychologists call 'pluralistic ignorance'. We look to see how others react; if they are not responding, we assume we have misinterpreted the situation. We don't want to look foolish, so we go with the majority position. But if everyone is doing this, and no one knows what is going on, the sufferer goes unaided.

CHAPTER 15

Are you the best 'you' that you can be?

Who are you? Who do you want to be? Are they the same thing?

Throughout history, philosophers and religious leaders have suggested how people might improve themselves and their lives. Now psychologists have joined in and a whole self-help book industry has sprung up, much of it feeding on our dissatisfaction and insecurity. So how can you make the most of yourself and your time on this Earth?

What is self-actualization?

The goal might be called enlightenment or salvation, personal fulfilment or – most recently – self-actualization. In any guise, it is about living your life well, with meaning and integrity. While religions often impose a preconceived notion of how to live virtuously, self-actualization is about fulfilling your potential, becoming the person you feel you should be or most want to be – the best version of 'you'. The ideal varies from person to person; it's an individual quest with no single script.

> '*What a man can be, he must be. This need we may call self-actualization. . . . It refers to the desire for self-fulfilment, namely, to the tendency for him to become actualized in what he is potentially. This tendency might be phrased as the desire to become more and more what one is, to become everything that one is capable of becoming.*'
>
> Abraham Maslow

The qualities of self-actualization

Maslow identified the following common features among the self-actualizers he studied:

- They had a realistic view of themselves and others and accepted people for what they were, tolerating flaws
- They were resourceful, independent and autonomous
- They saw reality clearly and judged situations honestly, in other words, they were not easily deceived
- They were spontaneous

- They tended to be unconventional and didn't slavishly follow established norms and conventions
- They could tolerate uncertainty
- They needed privacy and time to themselves
- They were highly creative
- They were centred on a task or problem outside themselves
- They had an unusual sense of humour that was not at the expense of others
- They had strong ethical standards by which they lived
- They appreciated the world and viewed it with a sense of awe and wonder
- They had deep, satisfying relationships with a few key people rather than a wide circle of shallow relationships
- They were concerned for the welfare of humanity
- They had 'peak experiences' (see box on page 122).

South African leader Nelson Mandela is an example of a highly self-actualized individual, whose whole life focused on the goal of freedom and equality for black South Africans.

The path to self-actualization

Achieving the goal of self-actualization should be straightforward; it only requires you to be truly yourself. Yet many of us find this very difficult. We are too concerned about what other people think, about needing to fit in and wanting to match the expectations of others. This desire for belonging is, after all, something that Maslow identified as a need.

Is a sense of belonging in conflict with the self-actualizer's need

PEAK EXPERIENCES

Maslow identified having 'peak experiences' as a characteristic of self-actualized people. These are episodes of intense pleasure or feeling of enlightenment and insight that come about when contemplating great art, beauty in nature, or making an intellectual discovery or other personal accomplishment. They are ecstatic, transcendental and might make the person feel part of a great connectedness of nature or spirituality. The beneficial effect endures after the peak experience has finished.

Peak experiences are sometimes categorized as religious and revelatory by those who have them, and Maslow suggested that all religions have come about as the result of the peak experiences of some individual prophet or 'seer'. Pharmacological research has reproduced the peak-experience effect with the psychotropic drug psilocybin, present in the 'magic mushrooms' that have been used in certain types of religious ritual for millennia.

not to be governed by the views and expectations of others? It's a source of tension, perhaps, but not of conflict. Self-actualizers may be aware of what is expected of them, but they have sufficient objectivity and clarity of vision to distinguish between expectations which are simply the result of unchallenged habits and those rooted in something more valuable and therefore worth meeting.

> '*I was in a sort of ecstasy, from the idea of being in Florence, close to the great men whose tombs I had seen. Absorbed in the contemplation of sublime beauty . . . I reached the point where one encounters celestial sensations. . . . Everything spoke so vividly to my soul. Ah, if I could only forget. I had palpitations of the heart, what in Berlin they call "nerves." Life was drained from me. I walked with the fear of falling.*'
> Stendhal, on viewing Giotto's frescoes in Florence, 1817. The ecstatic frenzy of a peak experience brought on by viewing art is sometimes referred to as 'Stendhal syndrome'.

First steps

Some steps towards self-actualization are easier to make than others. The ones that require you to step just outside your comfort zone, rather than turn the tide, will help build your self-actualizing muscle. An easy first step is to work hard and with full conviction at whatever you do. Experience everything fully and be open to pleasure and wonder from small sources – in other words, adopt a more childlike way of experiencing the world. It's easy to be cynical, to say you've seen enough sunsets or that you don't have time to stop and look at birds in flight. But why limit your enjoyment of life, even if most adults do?

Consciously take responsibility for yourself and your actions instead of seeking somewhere else to lay the blame. This might feel scary at first, but it will soon give you a feeling of strength. Embrace new experiences instead of sticking to what is known and safe. They don't have to be anything dramatic – even just trying something different on the takeaway menu will broaden your experiences and develop your confidence. Today, crispy garlic squid; tomorrow, extreme snowboarding!

The bigger steps

No one is going to criticize you for working hard or trying something new. But taking those steps which will (or you fear will) bring disapproval from those around you presents more of a challenge.

The first rule is to be honest. This is harder than it sounds as it means acting in accordance with your real feelings and beliefs. Suppose everyone at your workplace is turning up earlier and staying later in an effort to impress? Self-actualizers won't play this game. They will do their work efficiently and work the necessary hours to do their job well, but won't pretend to be doing more than they are doing or engage in an escalating game.

Honesty is the best policy

Self-actualization requires being honest with, and to, yourself. If there is something you always do but hate doing – whether it's visiting an unpleasant relative or cleaning the bathroom – admit that you don't like it. What would be the cost of not doing it? Perhaps the unpleasant relative dislikes the visits as much as you do? Perhaps you would rather pay someone else to clean your bathroom for you? Even if you decide to carry on as usual, because the visits are valuable to your relative and you can't afford or don't approve of employing a cleaner, once you have chosen your course of action and taken responsibility for it, it will become easier to accept. If you are still fighting against it, you've made the wrong choice – and there is always a choice. You *could* stop seeing the relative, but you might alienate your family, lose an inheritance or feel plagued by guilt. It's still a choice.

Perhaps you like something that others look down on, such as caravanning holidays, popular boy-bands or cheap souvenirs. So what? Embarrassment comes with caring what other people think of your harmless choices. Work out for yourself what you think and enjoy, without deferring to the preferences of others. That's not to say you need to dismiss their opinions or never listen to advice, but it's important to evaluate all you see and hear in the light of your own experiences and tastes and make your own choices – ones that will make you happy and fulfilled.

Stand firm

The hardest step is to stand up for the things you want and believe when they are different from those the people around you want and believe. It takes courage to remain true to your beliefs, to stand against the tide of opinion and face hostility. You might suffer for your beliefs, but if you are self-actualized it will be worth it because integrity will have become your greatest treasure. This explains why Nelson Mandela and Aung San Suu Kyi spent years in jail; and why Edward Snowden revealed the National Security Agency's secrets and was forced to flee the United States for Hong Kong and then Russia. These people believed in something greater than themselves, and thought it was worth the risk or suffering involved.

Self-actualizing is about your self

To be self-actualized, you need to know who you should be. This, by definition, is different for everyone. Someone can be lazy and rude but still self-actualized, if they have been true to their own values and aims. Diogenes might fall into that category. No

ACTUALIZATION

Abraham Maslow saw self-actualization as the pinnacle of human achievement. He put it at the top of his pyramid of needs (see Chapter 2), saying that it could only be attempted once all the lower needs, from food to self-esteem and endorsement by others, had been met. He claimed that only 1–2 per cent of people ever attain self-actualization, as most of us remain caught up in pursuing those pesky needs for food, shelter and a halfway decent car. But for Maslow, 'people' principally meant white American males of the mid-20th century, who really aren't most people (especially now). A quick assessment suggests that there are many people we regard as self-actualized who do not seem to have met some of the needs further down the pyramid.

Maslow acknowledged that not all people feel the needs in the order in which he put them and that, for some people, they may be met in a different order. This is encouraging, as it means you can still aim for self-actualization even if other people don't respect your views or you have a chronic health problem. There is some contradiction between Maslow's pyramid of needs and self-actualization. What he called 'belongingness' is manifested in the need for endorsement and respect from others. Yet one of the characteristics he identified in self-actualized people was the ability to persevere with views that were unpopular in spite of fierce opposition. If the views were securely held, it allowed people to leapfrog the bit of the pyramid that specified endorsement and respect from others.

one can do your self-actualizing for you, or tell you who it is you should be aiming to be.

The self-actualized are sympathetic to the needs of others to self-actualize, so they don't try to force their views on people or mould their children to their own ambitions. Instead, they help others to find their own path and endorse brave choices even if they are not the choices they would have made themselves.

Is it all good?

Self-actualization sounds like a commendable course of action but there can be problems with it, as Fritz Perls pointed out. Perls, the originator of Gestalt therapy, said there is a danger of people actualizing an ideal of the self, rather than the genuine self. We all have an idea of the type of person we want to be, and it is not always a good match for the type of person we are capable of being. Perls also felt there was a danger that self-actualization would be felt as an obligation, so it would bring undue pressure to bear upon the individual.

> '*Why do we set our standard of sanity so cautiously low? Can we imagine no better model than the dutiful consumer, the well-adjusted breadwinner? Why not the saint, the sage, the artist? Why not all that is highest and finest in our species?*'
>
> Theodore Rozsak, Professor of History, California State University, 1977

French national heroine Jeanne d'Arc possessed many of the qualities of the self-actualized. Some might describe her 'peak experiences' – mystical visions – as delusional, but they gave her the courage and conviction to lead an army of rebellion against the English.

Ironically, the pressure to conform to an ideal by being self-actualized (obedience) runs counter to the flouting of convention and social pressure if they don't coincide with your beliefs and inclinations (disobedience). Also, is it appropriate to regard a self-actualized person as morally 'better'? What about Perls' argument that a person's inability to self-actualize may be because his or her needs have not been met or there is a lack in some other capacity through no fault of their own? And while some might argue that a person is too lazy to improve him or herself, others might contend that the person's actualized self is unmotivated (and therefore 'lazy', to put a judgemental spin on it). So ,by this token, he is the best version of himself that he can be.

THE BEST VERSIONS OF THEMSELVES

Maslow's study of how to achieve self-actualization was based on the biographical details of 18 famous people he considered to be self-actualized. They included:

- Abraham Lincoln – US president
- Albert Einstein – physicist; Nobel Prize winner for Physics
- Eleanor Roosevelt – political activist working for the rights of women and African Americans
- William James – philosopher and psychologist
- Sigmund Freud – psychologist.

Carrot or stick?

Is the best way to motivate people by reward or punishment – or both?

People are impelled to act by two different forces. When we do something for our own reasons – because we enjoy the activity, find it rewarding in some way, or it builds towards goals which are valuable to us – we are internally motivated. If you like to bake, you won't need encouragement, you will be happy to do it. When we do something to control external circumstances, such as getting paid, avoiding going to jail or going hungry, and so on. we are externally motivated. If you have a job you don't much like, you will continue to turn up and do as you are told because you need the money you are paid for doing it. If you hate shopping for food, you will still do it because otherwise there won't be any food in the house when you are hungry. It's the external motivation that is subject to carrot-and-stick-ness.

Too many carrots spoil the broth?

In 1973, psychologists Mark Lepper, David Greene and Richard Nisbett carried out an experiment with a group of three- to five-year-old nursery schoolchildren to test the 'overjustification' theory of reward. They selected 51 children who enjoyed drawing. Each child was encouraged to draw for six minutes. The fact that the children already liked the activity was key to the study. Before starting, the children were randomly put into three groups. One group was promised a reward (a certificate) if they did some drawing. The other two groups weren't told this. After the session, those who had been promised it were given a certificate and children from one of the other groups also received a certificate. For this group, the reward was a surprise. The third group received nothing.

Over the next few days, the researchers observed the children and noted the amount of time they spent drawing of their own volition. The results were surprising. There was no statistical difference between those given a surprise reward and those given no reward, but those receiving the promised reward drew *less*.

It seems that for an activity we enjoy, internal motivation is enough. If external reward is added to that, we bump into 'overjustification', whereby an expected incentive (the certificate) decreases the person's intrinsic motivation to complete the task.

The children who were given the promised reward suddenly had an external explanation for their behaviour, which was that they were drawing in order to receive a reward. It followed that, if no reward was promised, they wouldn't do any drawing.

It appears we generally associate external rewards with actions we don't want to do. Children might be rewarded for tidying their toys away, cleaning their room, eating their greens or doing their homework. But think carefully before you plan to reward any of these actions. If your children like greens or homework, you might put them off by giving them a pudding or a star chart, because the reward suggests that the activity was something that shouldn't be liked. After all, why would we need to be rewarded for something we are internally motivated to do?

Overjustification works on adults too. People who are rewarded for giving up smoking are less successful than people who receive no reward. If their internal motivation is displaced by a less powerful external motivation, they are less likely to succeed.

What lies behind this is the self-perception effect (see Chapter 25). Our assessment of ourselves depends on how we behave. This sounds counterintuitive, as we would usually imagine that how we behave is manifest in how we think about ourselves. We tend to assume that our personality and attitudes drive our actions, when in fact the reverse is true. Our actions are often not the product of our own free will, as we might believe.

Why do bankers need massive bonuses?

Most people who are not bankers will wonder why bankers are paid massive bonuses for doing a job they are already paid handsomely to do. Studies of motivation and external reward show that if people are rewarded simply for completing a task, or doing it for a certain number of hours, their motivation is less than if they are rewarded for competence.

If you tell someone they are being paid for doing a task well, it will make them work harder and longer – regardless

BORING OR INTERESTING?

In 1959, Leon Festinger carried out an experiment at Stanford University in California which involved employing people to carry out a dull task. Afterwards the participants were paid either $1 or $20 to tell the next lot of participants that the task was interesting. When questioned later on, those who had been paid $20 said it was boring, but those who had been paid $1 rated it as more interesting.

Festinger's study was part of his work on cognitive dissonance (see Chapter 24). It showed that people would persuade themselves a task was more enjoyable than it was because they didn't want to admit they had wasted their time on it. Those who were paid more reported less favourably on the task. Generally we are paid to do things we don't want to do. If we are paid a reasonable amount to do something, it's a fair bet it's something we wouldn't choose to do otherwise. It's not a fun thing, so we shouldn't enjoy it. Conversely, the less we are paid, the more fun the task should be - apparently.

of whether they do the task well or not. The reason given for paying bankers exorbitant salaries and extravagant bonuses is that, without these rewards, they will leave their jobs in droves for richer pastures. It turns out that this is probably true (but it doesn't answer the question of why we don't just let them leave anyway).

The bankers' persistent denials that they are the cause of the economic crash are borne out by psychological theory. If a person is paid more for a task, he/she will believe they did it better and enjoyed it more than if they were paid badly for it. By paying bankers large sums we reinforce their belief that they are doing a good job and so we encourage them to continue.

Punishment works better than reward

The US economist John List tried different ways of motivating teachers to coach students to pass an exam. He told one group of teachers that they would receive a bonus if their students' test results improved. In another group, he gave each teacher $4,000, and said they'd have to give it back if their students' grades didn't improve. On average, the students of the second group of teachers scored 7 per cent higher than the students of the first group.

CHARITY AND ANTI-CHARITY

Some people try to coerce themselves to achieve goals by pledging to give money to charity if they fail – for example, they'll say that if they don't lose weight they will give money to fund cancer research. This method seldom succeeds.

While the incentive to hold on to one's money is a reasonable spur to action, the fact that the money is going to a good cause undermines the incentive. Giving money to worthy charities makes us feel good about ourselves and what we have done. This means that we are setting a punishment which will make us feel good. You miss your target, and think, 'Oh well, the money has gone to a good cause.'

It is much more effective to pledge to give to an anti-charity – a cause you don't support. It could be a political party or activist group you don't like, for instance. There is then a much more powerful incentive to succeed in doing what you set out to do.

CHAPTER 17

Can you spot a psychopath?

He or she won't necessarily be a knife-wielding maniac – so what are the less obvious signs?

Would you know a psychopath if you saw one? Well, you probably have seen at least one. It's thought that around 1–2 per cent of people could be classed as psychopaths. That also means there's a 1 per cent chance that you are a psychopath. There's no need to worry too much – not all psychopaths turn into killers. In order for them to do so, there needs to be a particular coincidence of genes and environmental triggers.

Natural-born killers?

Jim Fallon is a psychologist who studies the brains of psychopathic killers. He has found that underactivity in the orbital cortex, a part of the brain just above the eyes, is a universal feature of the psychopathic killers he has examined. In addition, they have abnormalities in the amygdalae, two small structures located deep within the brain involved in regulating emotions and morality. Typically, the amygdalae are underactive and around 18 per cent smaller in psychopaths than in non-psychopaths. The result is that psychopaths essentially have no conscience. Although they can tell that something is wrong by comparing it with a set of moral rules, they have little or no innate sense of wrong-doing.

A psychopath in the family

While working on psychopathy, Fallon was also examining PET scans of the brains of people with Alzheimer's disease. Since his mother's family had a history of Alzheimer's, he included scans from his family members in case he was able to spot some early signal. Fallon was reassured to find no evidence of Alzheimer's, but the last scan in the pile was an obviously psychopathic brain. He assumed he had mixed up his scans. But when he checked, he discovered that it was a scan of his own brain. He – the accomplished neuroscientist – had the brain of a potential psychopathic killer.

When he mentioned this to his mother, she suggested that he investigate his father's family. Fallon discovered that he was directly descended from seven killers including the first man to be executed for matricide in America. Another relative was Lizzie Borden, suspected of killing her father and stepmother with an axe in 1892.

Psychopathic genes

Fallon concluded from his studies that there are several genes, called 'warrior genes', which predispose to violent psychopathic behaviour. But the carriers of these genes don't become killers unless things also go wrong in their environment. He attributed his own relatively tranquil life to the love of his parents. According to Fallon, those who do become serial killers have usually been abused or suffered other extreme trauma in childhood. Something triggers their violence beyond the genetic predisposition.

Does capitalism need psychopaths?

So what of the 1 per cent of potential psychopaths walking the streets? Many of them are successful in business. Psychopathy is over-represented among CEOs, with an estimated 4 per cent having psychopathic traits. Fallon is a psychopath who is a successful neuroscientist. Pro-social psychopaths, such as Fallon, have less empathy than most other people, do not form close

*Lizzie Borden took an axe
And gave her mother forty whacks.
When she saw what she had done,
She gave her father forty-one.*

relationships easily, and are frequently highly competitive, but they seldom go around killing people.

When Fallon asked his friends and family to outline his personality, they all described him as sociopathic. He said that when he thought about it, he didn't care – and that proved they were right. A pro-social psychopath is often gregarious, hard-working, apparently sociable, but only at a fairly superficial level (they can be quite charming), but perhaps not the easiest person to have as a family member or close friend.

It's not clear whether psychopathy is a condition that people either have or don't have, or whether there is a collection of tendencies and behaviours that, in combination, result in psychopathic behaviour. If the latter, there will be a wide spectrum of psychopathy ranging from completely non-psychopathic to dangerous, criminal psychopaths.

Empathy disorders

The British psychologist Simon Baron-Cohen, an expert in empathy disorders, has noted that psychopaths are lacking in genuine empathy but are good at turning empathy on and off – they can plausibly emulate empathy while not actually

> *Serial killers ruin families. Corporate and political and religious psychopaths ruin economies. They ruin societies.'*
>
> Robert Hare, University of British Columbia

feeling or acting on consideration or fellow-feeling for others. People on the autistic spectrum also have 'zero empathy', but they struggle with 'theory of mind' – the ability to appreciate another person's point of view or feelings. Psychopaths are very good at understanding how others think, even if they don't share their feelings. This makes them proficient and ruthless manipulators.

Does faking madness make you mad?

The journalist Jon Ronson has studied and written extensively about psychopathy. During his research, he went to meet a man called Tony in the high-security mental health institution Broadmoor, in Berkshire, England. Tony told Ronson that he had been arrested for beating someone up in a bar when he was 17 and was advised by another prisoner to fake madness. He thought this would gain him a lighter sentence. Tony faked psychopathy, borrowing ideas from films and books. He told the authorities that he got sexual pleasure from crashing cars into walls, an idea taken from the movie *Crash*. He said he wanted to watch women die as it would make him feel normal – an idea taken from the autobiography of serial killer Ted Bundy. Tony was so convincing that instead of being sent to a cushy jail he wound up in the harshest secure institution in the land.

Even though Tony said he had only faked madness, he spent 14 years in Broadmoor before he was eventually released. Tony told Jon Ronson that every time he did something normal – talk to a nurse about an odd news story or wear a suit, for example – it was taken as evidence of madness. Ronson spoke to a clinician who concluded that although Tony had deliberately faked psychopathic symptoms, he was so lacking in remorse and so manipulative that he probably was psychopathic.

In the movie One Flew Over the Cuckoo's Nest *(1975), Jack Nicholson's character fakes madness to avoid hard labour.*

Despite his extensive studies of psychopathy, Ronson was fairly convinced by Tony. Was Tony a psychopath who manipulated Ronson into believing his story? Or perhaps he truly wasn't one. As Tony found out, it is easy to persuade someone you are mad, but much harder to prove you are sane. A lot of the things sane people do can look mad to others. Twenty months after his release, Tony was again jailed for attacking someone in a bar.

PSYCHOPATH CHECKLIST

There are numerous tests to assess the degree of psychopathy displayed by any individual. One of the most widely used is the Hare Psychopathy Checklist, which itemizes characteristics for which the subject is rated. Signs of psychopathy measured by the Hare checklist include:

- glib and superficial charm
- grandiose estimation of self
- need for stimulation
- pathological lying
- cunning and manipulativeness
- lack of remorse or guilt
- shallow affect (superficial emotional responsiveness)
- callousness and lack of empathy
- parasitic lifestyle
- poor behavioural controls
- sexual promiscuity
- early behaviour problems
- lack of realistic long-term goals
- impulsivity
- irresponsibility
- failure to accept responsibility for own actions
- many short-term marital relationships
- juvenile delinquency
- criminal versatility

CHAPTER 18

What do you see?

Your eyes and brain work together to see things, but the images they produce can be confusing.

Look at the image on page 137. You will have seen it, or one like it, a hundred times. Why does it appear to jump backwards and forwards between a vase and two faces? What is it doing to our brains to make this happen? The answer is that our brains like to work out what is the foreground and what is the background of an image; and when they can't – when both background and foreground make discrete meaningful shapes – we see something called a multi-stable image.

Patterning what we see

When we look at things, our brains have a lot of work to do to make sense of them. All the brain receives is a set of data in the form of coloured light emitted or reflected by objects 'out there'. To see in a meaningful way, the brain needs to recognize objects, even when they are differently lit, differently oriented and different distances from the eye.

So how much of seeing is learned and how much is innate? Experiments with very young babies (two to three months old) have shown that some of the brain's ability to process information is already in place. Constancy of size (recognizing that an object is a single size whether it is near or far away), the ability to view the world in three dimensions, and shape and pattern recognition are skills innate to most young babies. Jerome Bruner's studies in 1966 (see Chapter 26) on cognitive development showed that young children are active problem-solvers.

Seeing and moving

Experiments carried out on animals in the 1960s produced results which would impact on cognitive development studies thereafter. They revealed that a young animal deprived of normal light and patterns would not be able to respond normally to these stimuli later on in life. In 1963, R. Held and A. Hein found that if kittens were prevented from exploring their environment, they would later be unable to place their paws properly or respond to approaching objects. Held and Hein concluded that this was because the kittens had not been able to develop depth perception; they were therefore incapable of linking coordination and perception.

Studies of people who have their sight restored after losing it as a baby, and of those who have been blind from birth, suggest that some aspects of vision are learned and others are innate. Cultural differences, and the environment in which people grow up, can also affect perceptual abilities. Colin Turnbull studied the Mbuti pygmy group of Zaire. As the Mbuti people live in dense forest, Turnbull suspected they would have difficulty judging distance and size. He found that if he took Mbuti people to the plains and showed them a herd of buffalo in the distance, they thought them 'strange insects' and were amazed that the animals appeared to grow larger as they drew nearer.

> 'Whilst part of what we perceive comes through our senses from the object before us, another part (and it may be the larger part) always comes out of our own mind.'
>
> William James, philosopher and psychologist

Look for the whole, not the hole

Look at the image below:

Your mind organizes this design into a white triangle in front of three black circles, or a white triangle with black corners. It is less likely that you will just see three three-quarter circles. If we were to rearrange the components, however, it would be easy to see them.

The mind has a natural tendency to see the whole rather than the various elements, and the whole is more than the sum of the parts. It's a bit like comparing a salad with its ingredients. Nothing has happened to the ingredients – it's just how they are presented. If you came to my house and I gave you an avocado, a pile of rocket, some pine nuts, a chunk of parmesan, a bottle of virgin olive oil and some balsamic vinegar, you wouldn't be that impressed. But if I had mixed them together and made them look nice, you'd probably be quite happy with it.

Size and distance

Now look at the image below:

The brain interprets this image as a series of figures increasing in size from left to right, with the smallest closest to us. The lines suggesting walls and paving persuade us that this is a perspective view, and that the figure on the right is the more distant. Actually, these three figures are the same size. Your brain is doing the perspective work: if one figure appears to be in the distance and is the same size as a figure in the foreground, our brains tell us that the background figure should appear smaller. Therefore, if the figure in the distance appears to be the same size as the one in the foreground, our brains tell us that the figure in the background is larger.

What's missing?

Our brains automatically supply the missing parts to make a picture fit the patterns we are used to seeing. Look at the shapes below:

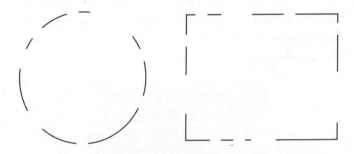

You see them first as a circle and a rectangle, not lots of different lines. But it's not just about seeing the whole. Our brains make lots of deductions and assumptions to help us interpret what we

see. Look at the photo on the right. Is this a pony shape painted onto a fence? Or is it the shadow of a pony which is standing just out of shot?

Your brain uses your knowledge and past experience to interpret what it sees. A young child who had never seen a pony-shaped animal might guess that this is a shadow because he or she is used to seeing shadows, but not accustomed to seeing odd shapes painted on fencing.

And what's there?

The image of a 'face' on Mars (below, top photo), released 40 years ago, prompted people around the world to propose various theories about aliens having visited the planet or lived on it in the past. Some even suggested that gods may have left imprints there. Then, in 1998, when images of the same topographical feature taken from a slightly different angle and under different lighting conditions were released, they revealed it to be just a mountain (below, bottom photo).

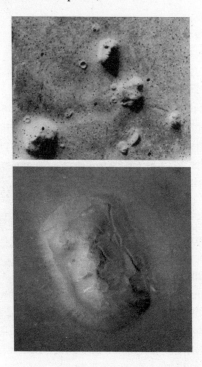

The brain has to recognize different objects so it can identify that two are the same type of thing, even if they don't look very similar. We have no difficulty identifying human beings, even though they can be tall, short, fat, thin, or whatever. Similarly we can easily recognize a tree or a chair or a cat, even if we have never seen that particular type of tree, chair or cat before.

We can also recognize the same object when seen from different angles, distances or positions. And even though our depth perception is usually created by using the input from both eyes, we don't see a two-dimensional image if we close one eye. Our brain compensates and makes a pretty good stab at creating a three-dimensional perspective view using the input from one eye.

PAREIDOLIA

Pareidolia is the phenomenon in which the brain finds significance or patterns in random images or sounds. The mind reinforces the familiar, struggles to find meaning, and comes up with patterns that don't reflect reality but give us a way of interpreting what we see or hear. Pareidolia explains why people visualize the Virgin Mary or Allah in toasted cheese sandwiches, or faces in place of mountains on Mars.

No undo function

You can't undo the work your brain has done in figuring out what it sees, unless a second interpretation is equally valid. Look at the image on the following page.

To start with, you will see a lot of black splodges. But the moment you perceive an actual image, it's very difficult to go back to seeing it as a random pattern.

Perhaps you can remember the time before you learned to read, when you saw writing only as a bunch of squiggles. Once you can read, it's impossible to see writing as mere shapes. To recapture that feeling, you have to look at a script in a language you aren't able to read. The image below shows some text in Tamil. Unless you read Tamil, you only see it as abstract shapes:

Parts or wholes?

Gestalt theory says we perceive things in their totality, not by putting the parts together. In the camouflaged picture of the Dalmatian dog on the facing page, we don't see the ears first, then the tail, then the paws and deduce from these that it's a Dalmatian. We see the whole dog at once (or not at all).

The white triangle in front of three black circles on page 139 is an example of reification – the way our minds add things that are not in the original image. Invariance is the property which tells us that an object is unchanged, even if viewed from a different angle or distance or differently represented (sometimes even distorted).

If you look at any walls spotted with various stains or with a mixture of different kinds of stones, if you are about to invent some scene, you will be able to see in it a resemblance to various different landscapes adorned with mountains, rivers, rocks, trees, plains, wide valleys, and various groups of hills. You will also be able to see divers combats and figures in quick movement, and strange expressions of faces, and outlandish costumes, and an infinite number of things which you can then reduce into separate and well-conceived forms.'

Leonardo da Vinci,
Notebooks

A question of perception: A and B show an object viewed from different angles. C shows the same object distorted. D shows different representations of the object.

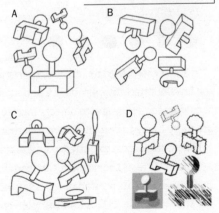

How we pattern things

Gestalt theory suggests that our minds follow certain laws which help us to impose patterns on what we see.

The law of proximity makes us see things as groups if they are close together. We see image A (below) as three groups of twelve circles rather than just 36 circles.

The law of similarity states that we tend to group things if they are similar. In image B (below) we see three rows of black circles and three rows of white circles, rather than a block of 36 circles.

A ○ ○   ○ ○   ○ ○
  ○ ○   ○ ○   ○ ○
  ○ ○   ○ ○   ○ ○
  ○ ○   ○ ○   ○ ○
  ○ ○   ○ ○   ○ ○
  ○ ○   ○ ○   ○ ○

B ○ ○ ○ ○ ○ ○
  ● ● ● ● ● ●
  ○ ○ ○ ○ ○ ○
  ● ● ● ● ● ●
  ○ ○ ○ ○ ○ ○
  ● ● ● ● ● ●

The law of symmetry is what makes us complete a partial triangle or other unfinished shape. It also makes us group objects by symmetry. So we see the following – [ ] { } [ ] – as three sets of brackets, not as six separate brackets.

In some cases, the law of past experience can overrule the laws of proximity, similarity and symmetry. If we are accustomed to seeing two objects next to each other, then we are more likely to perceive them together.

For example, past experience will make us see the following symbol – '13' – as the number thirteen. If, however, we are looking at a configuration of letters in which we expect to see the letter 'B' – 1313C, for example – we will recognize the configuration as the abbreviation 'BBC'.

The law of common fate makes us group objects if they move together or in the same direction.

The law of continuity is what makes you see the images below as two lines that cross rather than four lines that meet.

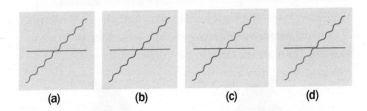

(a)   (b)   (c)   (d)

The law of 'good Gestalt' says that we perceive shapes and lines together if they form an object that is simple, regular and concise. Our mind tries to impose regular form on things we see. So we see the image on the right as a square and a triangle overlapping, not as an irregular shape with eight sides.

Verbatim and gist

One model of perception says that we encode what we see in two ways: verbatim and gist. Verbatim refers to what the image actually shows and gist refers to the meaning we take from it. This allows us to play tricks on our minds. Give an instant response – what colour is the text in this box above?

BLACK

US psychologist John Ridley Stroop took this a stage further. He discovered that if you print the names of colours in a different colour they took longer to read because the brain had to overcome its initial confusion. This delay in mental reaction times has since been exploited in countless psychological experiments. It is known as the 'Stroop effect'.

Bats out of hell

Often more than one type of pattern can be imposed on something ambiguous or incomplete that we see. Psychologists and recruitment staff sometimes use a certain test to gain some kind of insight into a person's preoccupations or character. Devised by Hermann Rorschach in 1921, the inkblot test consists of showing people symmetrical inkblots and asking them what they see. There are ten cards in the full Rorschach test.

Responses are coded, interpreted and used to diagnose possible psychiatric conditions or indicate personality types. The Rorschach test was extremely popular in the 1960s, remains so in Japan, and is still widely used in the USA, but it is widely distrusted and barely used at all in the UK. There have been several criticisms of its validity.

Another test commonly intended to give an insight into patterns of thought, preoccupations and levels of creativity is to present someone with a shape or line and ask them to incorporate it into as many different drawings as they can. You can try this one yourself. Using a circle, draw as many pictures as you can in two minutes.

CHAPTER 19

Do violent images make you aggressive?

It's often said that violence on screen leads to violent behaviour in real life. What is the evidence for this?

Does viewing aggressive behaviour on TV, the internet and in video games make people more violent? Or is it just that a large proportion of young men play video games, so a large proportion of young male killers will also play video games?

The argument that being a witness to violence leads to violent behaviour seems compelling.

Game over

In 2013, Aaron Alexis shot dead 12 people at a naval yard in Washington D.C., USA. The media latched on to the fact that Alexis had enjoyed playing the video game *Call of Duty*, and suggested it could have been a trigger for his crime. Anders Behring Breivik, who killed 77 people in Norway in 2011, says he practised his aim by playing *Call of Duty* and *World of Warcraft*. Like Breivik, Adam Lanza, one of the boys responsible for the shooting at Sandy Hook Elementary School, 'trained' by playing *Call of Duty*. Seung-Hui Cho, who killed 32 people at Virginia Tech University in 2007, was a keen player of the violent video game *Counterstrike*. After nearly every mass shooting, the media has cited corruption-by-video-game or corruption-by-movie-violence as a contributing factor.

> **'Life is a video game. Everybody's got to die sometime.'**
>
> The words of Devin Moore, a teenager from Alabama who was arrested for a minor traffic offence. He snatched a gun from a police officer, shot three officers and stole a police car to make his getaway. He said he had been influenced by playing *Grand Theft Auto* (GTA).

Testing aggression

In 1961, psychologist Albert Bandura set out to discover whether children copy role models who demonstrate violence. He and his colleagues at Stanford University recruited 72 young children, together with adult researchers to act as models. Before separating the children into groups, the researchers pre-tested them for levels of aggression to ensure an even distribution of behaviours between the groups.

The children were then divided into groups, each made up of 24 boys and girls. One group was teamed with an 'aggressive' adult model, another group was teamed with a 'non-aggressive' adult model, and a control group was given no adult model. The children were led individually into a playroom where there were toys in one corner, and a mallet, peg board and Bobo doll in another corner reserved for adults. (Bobo dolls are large, durable, inflatable dolls that can be knocked over but quickly spring back to an upright position.)

The children from the first group played with the toys for ten minutes. Then an adult model came in, played with the adult toys for a minute, then attacked the Bobo doll, hitting it with the mallet, punching and throwing it around, and abusing it verbally. After ten minutes, the adult left the room. The children from the second group also played with the toys while a second adult model entered the room and played quietly with the adult toys for ten minutes, ignoring the Bobo doll, and then left. The children in the control group played on their own for ten minutes.

Aggression arousal

The children were taken individually to a different playroom full of interesting toys. They were allowed to play for two minutes, after which the experimenter told them that they had been allowed to play with his very best toys. Then he said he had decided to reserve these toys for other children.

He told the children that they could play in the experimental room instead. The idea was to generate negative feelings by making the children anxious and cross. The children were returned to the experimental room and allowed to play there alone for 20 minutes, while they were secretly observed by the team of researchers.

Bandura found that the children who had observed the attack on the Bobo doll were much more likely to attack or verbally abuse the doll themselves. He found a significant difference between levels of aggression in this group: the girls were more physically aggressive if the model was male and more verbally aggressive if the model was female. Boys were more likely to imitate a male role model. Boys were three times more likely than girls to be physically aggressive, but there was little difference in verbal aggression between boys and girls.

Interestingly, the boys and girls who had been exposed to the non-aggressive role model were less likely to show aggression than children in the control group. It seems that a non-aggressive role model has a positive influence.

Findings

From these experiments, Bandura concluded that children learn social behaviour such as aggression through watching the behaviour of other people. This has significant implications for the effects of media violence on children.

However, it's not certain whether the positive and negative impact of watching the adult role models would have long-term effects on the children. Also, there was no relationship or communication between the children and the adult role models, which is not typical of the 'normal' modelling that takes place within the family.

It has also been suggested that the children were not acting out of aggression at all, but out of a desire to please by emulating the adult. It was later pointed out that children who had not played with a Bobo doll before were five times as likely to imitate aggressive behaviour than those who had grown used to playing with one.

The behaviour of the experimenter might also have encouraged aggression: the researchers had deliberately frustrated and taunted the children, which might itself be considered to be modelling aggression.

Vicarious reinforcement

Bandura repeated his experiment in 1963, this time to find out how reward and punishment affect whether children emulate aggressive behaviour. The first group of children witnessed a model aggressively attacking and screaming at a Bobo doll, and being rewarded with sweets. The second group saw the aggression being punished with the warning 'Don't do it again!' The control group saw no consequences meted out for the aggression.

The children were then allowed to play with the Bobo doll. The children who had seen aggression rewarded and those in the control group were more likely to be aggressive. The children who had seen aggression punished did not imitate it because they anticipated negative consequences.

Real life, film and cartoons

Bandura also compared his results with those of tests on children who had watched a real person act aggressively, children who had watched a film of someone attacking the Bobo doll, and a cartoon cat attacking the Bobo doll. In all cases, the children who had witnessed aggression, whether actual, on film or in a cartoon, were more likely to behave aggressively.

Tried and tested

Variations on the Bobo doll experiment have consistently produced similar results. When a live clown replaced the Bobo doll, the clown suffered at the hands of the children. When married men replaced children as the test subjects, and the attack on Bobo was replaced with violent or non-violent TV programmes, the men who watched the violent programmes were later reported by their wives to be more aggressive (1977). An experiment comparing the behaviour of people who watched a violent film with the behaviour of those who watched romantic movie produced similar results (1992).

There was also a difference in levels of aggression between people who played violent and those who played non-violent video games (2002). Those who played a violent video game were more aggressive afterwards than those who played a non-violent game.

Clearly, not all people who enjoy violent video games go on shooting rampages. Several of those who have carried out gun massacres were keen video gamers – but they were all young men, and many young men play video games. The Bobo doll experiments suggest there is a link between witnessing violence and acting aggressively, but this does not justify the assumption that playing violent games leads automatically to violent behaviour.

A link has been found between spending lots of time playing video games and depression. It's not clear whether gaming causes people to become depressed or that those prone to depression are more likely to play video games. Young teens (boys, principally) who spend many hours

'We went through something like 200 titles rented by the Venables family. There were some you or I wouldn't want to see, but nothing – no scene, or plot, or dialogue – where you could put your finger on the freeze button and say that influenced a boy to go out and commit murder.'

The words of a Merseyside detective who worked on the investigation into the murder of the toddler James Bulger by two older children in 1993. At the time it was suggested that the murder was linked with 'video nasties' – unclassified violent films released on video.

'Exposure to violence in video games may influence the development of moral reasoning because violence is not only presented as acceptable but is also justified and rewarded.'

Mirjana Bajovic,
Brock University,
Ontario, Canada

In 2006, the Indiana University School of Medicine carried out brain scans on 44 young people directly after they had played either a violent or a non-violent video game. Those who had played violent games showed extra activity in the amygdalae, (which, as we have already seen, are responsible for stimulating emotions) and decreased activity in the prefrontal lobe (which regulates self-control, inhibition and concentration). Those who had played non-violent games showed no such changes.

Numerous studies have found that watching something violent or threatening on screen causes a rush of adrenaline – the chemical that prepares the body to fight or flee when confronted with real-life peril. The body, at least, is not able to tell the difference between real violence and fantasy violence. When neither response is needed, the body is left awash with adrenaline which could make an aggressive response to some other trigger more likely.

a day playing video games of any kind often fall behind in developing social skills because they are not interacting with people in the real world. It's a chicken-and-egg situation: are asocial boys drawn to gaming or do gamers fail to develop social skills, and therefore become asocial? A study at Brock University in Canada found that children aged 13 and 14 who spent three hours or more each day playing violent computer games were slower to develop empathy and a sense of moral duty towards others than children not immersed in violent games. But, again, violent games might appeal more to people who are slower to develop empathy.

Moving on

Since Bandura's studies in the 1960s, violence in films and on TV has become even more graphic, and ever more violent video games have emerged. Violent video games are different from violent films and TV programmes in one important respect – the player is involved in perpetrating, not just viewing, simulated violence. Are these games, as some people claim, a safe outlet that facilitates the expression of violent feelings harmlessly? Or do they lead to an increased tendency for people to commit violence in the real world?

There have been dozens of further studies on the impact of watching real, video or cartoon violence since Bandura's experiments more than 50 years ago. There is still no consensus.

What did you come in here for?

Our memory can play tricks on us – but sometimes we play tricks on it as well.

We have all had the experience of entering a room for something and then forgetting what we went in there for. Or of being introduced to six people at a meeting or party and being unable to remember their names only a minute later. Short-term memory loss gets worse with age, but our short-term memories are not very good to start with. It's just that our memory's definition of short-term is even shorter than we think.

Do you remember when . . . ?

We can remember some things for a split second and some for a lifetime. Many things are forgotten altogether – at least consciously. Some 'forgotten' memories can be restored with hypnosis or other help. How does memory work?

Our eyes and ears store a snapshot of incoming data for less than a second. It's possible that this is used to decide which bits need to be moved to longer-term storage and which can be ignored. After all, our brains are subjected to a constant barrage of information, most of which is not needed.

Anything that looks useful is moved into short-term memory (STM). This is the type that should let you remember you went to the kitchen to pick up a spoon, or the name of the person you just met. STM typically lasts 15–30 seconds, so if your kitchen is a long way from where you started, that's why you forgot the spoon. STM can hold around seven items. If we deliberately try to remember things for a short time, we often do it by repeating words in our heads. STM seems to be acoustic, which may be why it is harder to remember words or sounds that are similar, such as rhyming words ('bat, cat, mat, rat, hat, and fat', for example) than to remember dissimilar-sounding words ('cat, dog, ham, toad, stick and mud').

Long-term memory (LTM) can store information for a whole lifetime. 'Can' store doesn't mean it always does, as anyone who has struggled to revise for an exam will know. LTM seems to have a limitless capacity – though it doesn't always seem like it. It is semantic – it works with meaning. It's easier for LTM to store similar-sounding words than words with similar meanings.

In 'Kim's game', taken from a Rudyard Kipling story, you look at a selection of items on a tray for 30 seconds, then look away and try to name them all. Most people who play this game can remember between five and nine items.

Often, we need to keep things in long-term memory for only a few minutes or hours. You might want to remember a shopping list until you get to the supermarket, but you won't need to recall it next year. After it's been used, you can safely forget it.

Why don't you forget how to ride a bicycle?

There are several types of memory. One, called procedural memory, is the type that's responsible for 'knowing how' to do something, such as a physical skill, and it's very resilient. Procedural memory stores all kinds of skills that, once learned, are rarely forgotten, including how to ride a bicycle. Even people who suffer anterograde amnesia, losing the ability to store long-term memories, usually remember the skills they have acquired, and can learn new skills of this type.

Other types of memory are imagery memory and declarative memory. What we see and hear forms imagery memories, which we can often recall just as we first experienced them. Declarative memory is the type we most often mean when we talk about memory. It includes semantic memory, which is responsible for recalling meaning and facts, and episodic memory, which is constructed from our personal history and is linked to particular times and places.

How we remember

Although the sequence sensory memory > short-term memory > long-term memory is fairly secure, it's very clear that not all we see, hear or experience makes it into long-term memory. Much of our time at school is spent trying to learn and remember things; making the right choice about what to remember is vital.

MEMORY TIP: CHUNKING

If you have to remember a number longer than seven digits, it's easier if you 'chunk' it. So a phone number is best remembered in pairs or triplets (or 'chunks'):

07 32 98 56 44

This is easier to remember than individual figures:

0 7 3 2 9 8 5 6 4 4

And a shopping list is easier to remember as: beans and bread; tomatoes and butter; coffee and milk, especially if there is some semantic meaning to the groups. (So coffee and milk is easier to remember than 'coffee and tomatoes' because people often put milk in their coffee but seldom tomatoes.)

A better way of looking at STM is considering it 'working memory'. If we compared it to a computer, sensory memory would supply the input from the keyboard and mouse, working memory would be RAM, and long-term memory would be the hard disk or cloud storage where we save our work.

Working memory has the task of processing incoming data and deciding whether to keep it or throw it away. Something called the 'central executive' operates as a sort of overseer or manager, juggling input and output. It can manage several tasks at once as long as they don't require the same types of skill or attention. So a person can knit and watch television, but not read and talk at the same time.

The bits and pieces that the working memory has singled out for long-term storage are best remembered if they are processed deeply. This means they must be analysed and understood, not just repeated. Repetition can work – it's how we learned the alphabet, and we don't forget it – but processes that give meaning or link new knowledge to existing knowledge are best for forming long-term memories.

WHAT WERE YOU DOING WHEN KENNEDY WAS SHOT?

Flashbulb memories are vivid fragments of episodic memory that burn themselves into the mind. They preserve intense moments for us personally, or our personal circumstances – what we were doing, where we were – when some dramatic or important event occurred. That's why lots of older people can tell you exactly what they were doing when they heard President Kennedy had been shot in 1963, or Martin Luther King, Jr in 1968, and many of us can remember what we were doing when we heard about the 9/11 terrorist attacks. (Not all psychologists agree that 'flashbulb' memories are anything special. They might seem very solid just because we revisit and rehearse them frequently.)

Surprise!

Things are more memorable if there is something distinctive about them. Complexity (as long as it's not so complex we don't understand) can aid recall. We are more likely to remember 'In Xanadu did Kubla Khan a stately pleasure dome decree' than 'Kubla Khan built a nice palace in Xanadu' (though the rhythm also helps). Anything distinctive is easier to remember.

Things are easier to remember if they have personal relevance. So if someone told you the meaning of a new word, you might remember it. If they asked whether a word applied to you, then explained what it meant, you would be more likely to remember it. So – 'corpulent' means fat. Are you corpulent? You might be offended by the question, but at least you will remember it. Even manufacturing a link might work.

Structuring memories

If you were to throw all your belongings – books, clothes, saucepans, DIY tools, sheets, everything – into one huge box, life would be very difficult. You would have to sort through all the hammers, phone chargers and onions every time you wanted a sock. Instead, we organize our possessions.

Our memories are the same. If memory just held a vast soup of car registration numbers, family holidays, chemical formulae and statistics about World War I, it would be hard to recall anything we wanted. So the brain uses schemas to structure what we know and remember. The application of schemas to the way we think was proposed by British psychologist Frederic Bartlett in 1932 and has been widely adopted and adapted.

You could think of a cutlery tray as a schema for cutlery. New information is easier to deal with if you can fit it into an existing schema. When you get a new spoon, you know where to put it. If you want a fork, you know where to look. Information that doesn't fit into a schema might be distorted, or easily forgotten, or mis-remembered. If it's important enough, we might revise the schema, but we are generally resistant to that. If someone gave you an ice-cream scoop and there was no space in your cutlery tray for ice-cream scoops, you might classify it as a spoon, or keep it in a different place, or decide you don't need one and get rid of it.

Not what you thought

The strong disposition of the mind to use schemas leads to our memories distorting information. It might be distorted to fit a schema when we first encounter it, and further distorted to fit better as our schemas develop and change over time. One way this manifests is through prejudice.

Suppose you see two people struggling in the street, a young man in a hoodie and an elderly woman. The elderly woman is holding a knife. You might well report later that the young man in the hoodie was holding the knife, because you would consider that to be the more likely scenario.

Bartlett investigated the impact of schemas on reliability of memory by telling a group of students a Native American folk tale, *The War of the Ghosts* (see box on page 166), and then having them recall and retell the tale several times over a year. They all believed they were retelling the story accurately, but made changes such as:

- missing out information irrelevant to them
- changing details, order and emphasis to match what seemed important to them
- rationalizing and explaining details that didn't seem to make sense
- changing the content and style to be more in keeping with the students' own cultural background.

Schemas affect our memories of situations and places, too. In 1981, Brewer and Treyens asked 30 people to wait, separately, for 35 seconds in a room which they were told was the office of an academic. They were later asked to recall what was in the office. Most correctly recalled things they expected to find in an office, such as a desk, but forgot unexpected objects (such as pliers). Some falsely recalled objects such as books and pens which they expected to be in an office but were not there. Bizarre unexpected items – including a skull – were well-remembered.

Don't forget

We might forget things from long-term memory if there is interference from other similar information encountered earlier or later. This confusion increases with the volume of information rather than the passing of time, at least over relatively short periods. It's not clear whether information is actually displaced from long-term memory, or fades away, or whether we just can't access it. It's quicker to re-learn something we have forgotten than to learn something completely new, so perhaps the information is still stored but we just can't reach it without renewing some link to it.

We are more likely to remember things if we revisit the context in which we first encountered or learned them. So divers who have memorized a list of words underwater are more likely to recall them underwater than on land. When people train in emergency techniques, they are more likely to remember them in a real emergency if they first practised them in a simulated emergency.

Could try harder

If you really want to remember something – when revising for an exam, for instance – you will have better recall if you:

- Repeat the material, as going over it three times (at least) will help to fix it in the long-term memory
- Elaborate on it, explaining it so that it makes sense to you
- Fit it into a context or schema so that it becomes part of your knowledge base
- Memorize cues that will help you to recall it, such as making up a mnemonic or fitting words to a tune.

WHEN FORGETTING IS GOOD FOR YOU

Sigmund Freud believed a source of anxiety and distress for many people is suppressed unpleasant memories from childhood. He thought the mind deliberately forgets or represses trauma as a protective mechanism. Such forgetting comes at a cost, though. To heal the anxiety or depression it causes, patients need help from a psychotherapist to uncover and deal with the suppressed memories. There has been some disagreement about whether recalling past trauma is helpful or harmful. Also, some 'uncovered' memories might be fabrications, suggested by the process of analysis or constructed from the patient's schemas.

The long-term memory responsible for learning motor skills is very resilient.

THE WAR OF THE GHOSTS

One night two young men from Egulac went down to the river to hunt seals. They heard war cries, and thought: 'Maybe this is a war party.' They escaped to the shore and hid behind a log. Then they heard the noise of paddles, and saw a canoe coming towards them. There were five men in the canoe, and they said: 'We wish to take you along. We are going up the river to make war on the people.'

One of the young men said, 'I have no arrows.'

'Arrows are in the canoe,' said the five men.

'I will not go along. I might be killed. My relatives do not know where I have gone. But you,' said the first young man, turning to the other, 'may go with them.'

So one of the young men went, but the other returned home. And the warriors went on up the river to a town on the other side of Kalama. The people came down to the water and they began to fight, and many were killed. Presently the young man heard one of the warriors say, 'Quick, let us go home: that Indian has been hit.'

The young man thought: 'Oh, they are ghosts.'

He did not feel unwell, but the others said he had been shot. So the canoes went back up the river and the young man went to his house. And he told everybody: 'Behold I accompanied the ghosts, and we went to fight. They said I was hit, and I did not feel sick.'

He told it all, and then he became quiet. When the sun rose he fell down. Something black came out of his mouth. His face became contorted. The people jumped up and cried. He was dead.

CHAPTER 21

Mind answering a few questions?

The techniques people use to get our attention are easy to spot when you know what to look for.

Lots of people want to persuade you to do things you don't really want to do. They need to develop more and more cunning techniques as they compete for your attention and compliance. So how does persuasion work, and can it be dangerous?

Have you had an accident?

Most people are plagued by nuisance phone calls. The caller – working in a call centre somewhere – doesn't know you, knows little about you, but has to try to get your attention before you put the phone down. If you hang up immediately, they've lost. But if they can get you to talk at all, they're in with a chance.

They might start by being especially polite, asking if you're having a nice day. If you answer the question, you are making an investment in the call and starting to build a bond with them. It's harder to put the phone down on someone you've just responded to.

They might then launch in to a fabricated story, 'I hear someone in your house has had a minor accident . . . ' Don't worry that your personal information has been leaked, or assume they have any information at all. They say that to everyone, and some of the people will have had an accident. The fact that they 'know' something about you makes you feel involved already – again, you're less likely to put the phone down. And if you haven't had an accident, the quicker you put the phone down the better, as you're taking up time they could be using to sell their accident solution to someone else.

They might say they are conducting a survey and ask you to help for a few minutes. Many people like to be helpful. And many people like answering questions about themselves (that's why we fill in silly quizzes in magazines and on websites). As soon as you agree to answer a few questions, you're on the hook. Now you've invested in the transaction and will not want to write off the time you've put into it.

A FOOT IN THE DOOR

An age-old technique of salespeople is 'foot in the door'. It's the same in principle as the 'will you help me with a survey?' approach. It gets its name from the door-to-door salesmen frequently encountered in the 1950s and 1960s, hawking everything from encyclopaedias to vacuum cleaners. They would, it's said, put their foot in the way of the door as the uninterested householder tried to slam it in their face. That foot gave them the chance to start their spiel and once they got going, they had the chance of a sale.

Every time you stop to talk to a researcher or charity collector in the street, stay on the phone to a cold-caller or agree to take a leaflet, you are letting someone put a foot in the door.

Aren't you nice?

However uninterested you are in whatever product they will try to sell you further down the line, you've shown them and – more importantly – you have shown yourself that you're a helpful person. We like to think of ourselves as helpful. You feel good about yourself – you have helped this person do their job just by answering some questions. Now that you feel virtuous, and connected to the person who produced the good feeling by asking a favour of you, you won't want to spoil that good feeling by dropping out of the interaction. You will now want, even if ever so slightly, to keep it going.

Ask for a little, get a lot

A lot of persuasion plays on how we like to think of ourselves. In 1976, Robert Cialdini and David Schroeder carried out a study into charitable giving. Students working as charity collectors went door-to-door asking for donations for the American Cancer Society. Some just asked for the donation, but others added that 'even a penny helps'. They found that those who added the line about the penny collected more money. People responded by thinking, 'I can't give only a penny', so they gave more. Being so stingy as to give only a penny didn't fit with their self-perception as kind and generous people. By prompting people to think 'I can't give only a penny', the collectors have planted the idea that the prospective donors will give something – then it just becomes a matter of how much.

Catch their interest

Another technique is to pique people's interest. In 1994, Santos, Leve, and Pratkanis set a female researcher the task of standing on a street corner asking passers-by for change. When she just asked for change, 44 per cent of people gave money. When she asked for a quarter, 64 per cent of people complied, but this rose to 75 per cent when she asked for an odd amount such as seventeen or thirty-seven cents. Because it was more unusual, the request didn't elicit an automatic response – people stopped to think, and then, having become interested, they gave.

Not that much!

The opposite technique is to ask for a large favour and then, when the person refuses, to ask for a smaller one. The trick is to make the thing you *really* want the smaller favour.

Imagine you want a friend to collect your child from school one day. If you start by asking if she will take the child for the whole weekend while you go away, she's likely to say no. But if you follow up your request by asking if she will just collect him from school and bring him home, she will probably say yes. If someone makes a concession, we are likely to make a concession in return. It's easy to manipulate this situation to get what you want.

It's well known that if you phrase a request in such a way that people have an easy get-out, they'll take it. So if you say, 'I don't suppose you have time to give me a lift to town?' the default answer is 'No'. But if you hitch what you want on to a request for something you don't expect, you stand a good chance of getting the lesser favour. If you strike it lucky, you may even get the big favour. So the following – 'I don't suppose you would like to drive me to Birmingham, but could you please give me a lift to the station so that I can catch the train?' – might get you your lift to town.

Low-ball technique

As a sales pitch, you'd that increasing the request would be a disaster. But, surprisingly, it works. It's a technique typically associated with car sales. You show interest in a car, you're told the price, you decide to buy it. Then all the extras creep in, the price rising and rising. You still buy the car. Budget airlines do it, too. You've clicked on the tickets you want, and suddenly all kinds of supplements and optional extras start to appear, pushing the price up. In both cases, if we feel we've made a commitment, we follow through.

Forbidden fruit and reactance

Sometimes we don't want to persuade people to do or want something, we want to persuade them *not* to. This can be very hard to do, since as soon as something looks forbidden or dangerous, we want it. We don't like restrictions on our actions, and anything that looks like a restriction can produce a 'reactance' response – a reaction against the request or advice.

Brad Bushman and Angela Stack researched the impact of warning and information labels on how people responded to violent TV programmes and high-fat foods.

There are two conflicting responses to warning labels. 'Tainted fruit' theory suggests that if high-fat food is explicitly labelled as bad for us, we will avoid it. 'Forbidden fruit' theory suggests that we want what we think we shouldn't have. Researchers investigated the effects of no labelling, of information labels (which just gave facts), and of warning labels (which gave facts and pointed out risks). They found that high-reactance individuals found the warning labels attractive. They were more likely to want to watch a violent programme or eat a high-fat food labelled with warnings than one just giving information. Information labels trust you to use your judgement; but warning labels tell you what to do, and we don't like that.

Does power corrupt?

You might imagine you would be a benign ruler, but can you be sure?

We see it time and again: someone seems honourable when they enter public office, but within a short space of time they are acting like a corrupt tyrant. Apparently decent soldiers head off to war and within weeks they're napalming innocent villagers, raping young girls, manning the gas chambers or torturing Iraqi prisoners. Are they the few bad apples that spoil the barrel, as US Secretary for Defense Donald Rumsfeld said (of Abu Ghraib)? Or is the barrel spoiling the apples?

Recruiting prisoners

When Phil Zimbardo set up an experiment at Stanford University into the behaviour of people put into the role of prison guard or prisoner, he intended it to last two weeks. He wanted to find out how positions of authority or subservience affect behaviour. As he termed it, if you put good people into a bad situation, what do they do? In the end, he curtailed the experiment after only six days as the effects on his subjects were intolerable.

Phil Zimbardo's experiment was conducted in 1971, ten years after Stanley Milgram's chilling findings on obedience (see Chapter 2). Zimbardo advertised in the press for volunteers to take part in a psychology experiment into the effects of prison life. Of the 70 volunteers, he chose 24 candidates who were deemed normal and not at risk of psychological damage, and randomly assigned them the role of guard or prisoner. All were male students from the USA or Canada.

Playing the game – prisoners

The experiment started with realistic scenarios of arrest. The police (who were cooperating with the experimenters) arrived at the homes of 'prisoners' early one Sunday morning, searched and handcuffed them, bundled them into police cars and drove them away, often under the gaze of neighbours who assumed the whole thing was real. It was a high-stress start, emulating the experience of many real suspects as closely as possible.

The 'prisoners' were taken to a real police station, booked by real police officers wearing sunglasses, and then fingerprinted, photographed, blindfolded and left in a cell.

The 'prison' was an adapted corridor in the psychology department on the Stanford University campus. Ordinary lab doors were replaced with doors with steel bars, and the 'exercise yard' was the closed corridor. There were no windows or natural light, and no clocks. Prisoners were escorted to and from the toilet as necessary. A cupboard, dubbed 'the hole' and just large enough for a prisoner to stand upright in, was available for solitary confinement. It was 60cm square. As each prisoner arrived, he was told of the severity of his crime, then stripped, searched and sprayed with de-lousing spray. It sounds barbaric, but it was copied from procedures in a jail in Texas.

Each prisoner was dressed in a smock, with his prison number on the front and back. He was allowed no underclothes. That part was not copied from common prison practice, but calculated to produce a similar level of humiliation and dehumanization as routine prisons. The prisoners wore a chain around one ankle at all times. Instead of having his head shaved (as in reality), each man had to wear a cap made of a cut-down stocking. Prisoners were referred to, and had to refer to each other, by number and not by name. They slept three to a cell in barren rooms with just space for their beds.

Playing the game – guards

Guards were given no special training, but were told to use whatever methods seemed reasonable to maintain order in the prison. They were warned of the seriousness of their position and the dangers involved. They wore identical khaki uniforms and mirrored sunglasses, and had a whistle around their necks and 'billy clubs' (batons) borrowed from the police. Nine guards worked in shifts, three on shift at a time, looking after nine prisoners split between three cells. The extra guards and prisoners were on standby.

Playing the game – prison life

At 2.30am on the first night, the prisoners were awakened by a whistle and had to leave their cells for a 'count'. Counts happened regularly thereafter, day and night, as a way of getting guards to assert authority over prisoners. Guards were allowed to punish prisoners if they disobeyed orders or rules.

One common punishment was forcing prisoners to do push-ups. Zimbardo noted that Nazi concentration camp guards had also ordered prisoners to do this. One of Zimbardo's guards stepped on the prisoners' backs while they did push-ups, or made other prisoners sit or step on the backs of their fellows.

Rebellion

The first day, prisoners were compliant. The second day, they rebelled. They tore off their caps and the numbers from their gowns, barricaded themselves in their rooms and taunted the guards. The guards called for reinforcements and let off fire extinguishers at the prisoners to drive them away from the doors. (The fire extinguishers were intended for fire-fighting and not supplied for use as weapons.) The guards opened the cell doors, stripped the prisoners naked and forced the ringleader into solitary confinement. They harassed the other prisoners.

Privilege vs punishment

The team realized they couldn't continue to use nine guards to control nine prisoners. So they met and decided on methods of psychological rather than physical control. The three prisoners who had played the least part in the rebellion were moved into a 'privilege cell', given back their clothes, and allowed special food which they were told to eat in front of other prisoners who were not allowed to eat at all. A little later, some of the 'good' and 'bad' prisoners were swapped round, without explanation. The aim was to break solidarity between the prisoners – divide and rule, in other words. It worked: the prisoners became distrustful of one another, suspecting that some of the swapped 'bad' prisoners had acted as informants. Similar techniques, often making use of racial tension, were being employed in American jails at the time, according to the ex-convict consultants employed to advise the experimenters.

The response to the rebellion not only broke solidarity between the prisoners, it also built solidarity between the guards who now saw the prisoners as a threat to themselves as a group. They started to control the prisoners more rigorously, withholding toilet visits and then not allowing prisoners to empty their slop buckets, and controlling access to cigarettes.

Breaking down

Just 36 hours in to the experiment, one prisoner started to break down. He started to act irrationally, cry uncontrollably, and go into a rage. The prison consultant criticized the prisoner for being weak and explained the sort of abuse he could expect if he were a genuine prisoner. He offered the prisoner the chance of leniency in exchange for becoming an informant. It took a little while, and a lot more irrational behaviour, before the experimenters realized the man was in genuine distress and he was removed from the experiment. The experimenters were later startled to see that their own thinking had become attuned to the prison situation – they had assumed he was trying to con them and had not recognized genuine distress.

The experimenters were slipping into the role of prison superintendents too thoroughly. When rumours of a planned mass break-out began to circulate, instead of watching and noting the patterns of behaviour, the experimenters consulted with experts on prison security and worked out a plan to foil it. When Zimbardo asked the local police if he could move his prisoners into real holding cells for the night of the planned escape, his request was refused. He reacted angrily, chaining the prisoners together, putting bags over their heads and moving them to another area. Then he sat in the empty jail, waiting to confront the people who were going to spring his 'prisoners'.

A fellow psychologist, passing by, saw him and asked about the experiment, and then asked what the independent variable was. Zimbardo became angry, saying he had more important things to deal with. It was much later that he realized the experiment had got to him, too.

As it turned out, the break-out had been a rumour. Frustrated at their waste of time and their humiliation, the guards harassed and punished the prisoners in retaliation (retaliation for not trying to escape!). They made them clean toilet bowls with their bare hands, and forced them to perform humiliating acts, including simulated sodomy, and do strenuous exercise.

ALL TOGETHER NOW . . .

When parents were allowed to visit their sons who were taking part in the experiment, they made formal complaints about the treatment of their children but acted with deference towards the authority figures. Although they knew it was an experiment and had not personally agreed to be part of it, they were unwittingly playing the role the situation had assigned them.

The game's up

When Zimbardo held hearings for prisoners eligible for parole, two remarkable things happened. The ex-convict consultant who had taken the part of head of the parole board acted, to his own horror, just like the man who had refused his own requests for parole for 16 years. And the prisoners, when asked if they would surrender the money they had earned in the experiment in exchange for parole, mostly said they would – but then obediently returned to their cells while their appeals for parole were considered. Any of them could have opted out of the experiment immediately (forfeiting their fee), but they acted like real prisoners. It simply didn't occur to them to quit.

The experiment came to an end when a female psychologist (alone out of 50 external visitors) expressed horror at the way the young men were being treated. Zimbardo realized she was right, and halted the experiment after just six of its scheduled 14 days. Later, Zimbardo said they should have stopped earlier, after the second breakdown, but even the experimenters had been drawn in and taken over by their roles as prison officials. Scary stuff.

Bad apples or bad barrels?

By the end of the period, Zimbardo noted that there were three types of guard:

- 'Tough but fair' guards who treated the prisoners according to the rules
- 'Good guy' guards who did little favours for the prisoners and never punished them
- 'Bad guy' guards who were vindictive, sadistic and inventive in the forms of humiliation and punishment they came up with. They seemed to relish the power they held over the prisoners and wielded it at every opportunity. Hidden cameras revealed them abusing prisoners at night, for no particular reason, when they thought they were unobserved.

'I got really angry at him. Here I had a prison break on my hands. The security of my men and the stability of my prison was at stake, and now I had to deal with this bleeding-heart, liberal, academic, effete dingdong who was concerned about the independent variable! It wasn't until much later that I realized how far into my prison role I was at that point — that I was thinking like a prison superintendent rather than a research psychologist.'

Phil Zimbardo, experimental psychologist

Zimbardo found nothing in the profiles of the 'good guy' or 'bad guy' guards which could have led him to predict which they would be.

The prisoners, too, fell into groups. Some were compliant, keeping out of trouble by obeying instantly; others put up a fight. There were more hints from the prisoner profiles of how they would behave. Those used to a more disciplined life were better able to withstand the pressures of being a prisoner and held out for longer than the others.

A foreshadowing of Abu Ghraib

Zimbardo has noted the similarities between the conditions meted out in his experiment and in the US military prison Abu Ghraib in Iraq. Some of them are quite startling.

In Abu Ghraib, prisoners were stripped and made to stand with bags on their heads. The faking of humiliating sexual acts was a tactic used in both Stanford and Abu Ghraib. The abuse in Abu Ghraib was blamed on 'a few bad apples', but Zimbardo has argued that it is not the case that bad apples spoil the barrel, but that perhaps that bad barrels spoil the apples. The situations we put people in can either make or allow them to do bad things.

Years after the experiment, Zimbardo spoke as an expert witness at the trial of the Abu Ghraib guards. Of course, the guards in Abu Ghraib really were under stress – they were in a conflict situation, dealing with people who they believed wanted to kill them. The 'guards' in Stanford had no such excuse. When the experiment was suspended, the prisoners were – unsurprisingly – pleased. Many of the guards, though, were disappointed. Even among the 'good' guards, none had objected to the way in which the prisoners were being treated. Not a single person except the lone visiting female psychologist had sounded a note of concern on behalf of the prisoners.

> *'I don't regard it as an experiment or a simulation because it was a prison run by psychologists instead of run by the state. I began to feel that that identity, the person that I was that had decided to go to prison was distant from me — was remote until finally I wasn't that, I was 416. I was really my number.'*
>
> 'Prisoner Number 416', a volunteer in the Stanford Prison Experiment

The power of evil?

The experiment would not be allowed today. It would not pass an ethics committee. There was danger of serious psychological damage both to prisoners and guards – and, as it turned out, to the experimenters who became so caught up in their own experiment that even they lost sight of its fiction.

It might seem that this is similar to Milgram's experiment (see Chapter 12), but there are significant and chilling differences. Milgram's experiment tested whether people would obey others and inflict harm – whether we can be enlisted into cruelty when there is a figure of authority taking responsibility for the outcomes.

It's bad enough that people are willing to deliver near-fatal electric shocks to innocent others just because they are told to. But the Stanford Prison Experiment was even more disturbing. Zimbardo has used the word 'evil' to describe what people would do to one another. The title of his book about the experiment is uncompromising: *The Lucifer Effect: Understanding How Good People Turn Evil*. The experiment uncovered a dark aspect of human nature – people's willingness to harm

> 'If only there were evil people somewhere insidiously committing evil deeds, and it were necessary only to separate them from the rest of us and destroy them. But the line dividing good and evil cuts through the heart of every human being.'
>
> Alexander Solzhenitsyn, *The Gulag Archipelago*, 1973

> 'Any deed that any human being has ever committed, however horrible, is possible for any of us – under the right circumstances. That knowledge does not excuse evil; it democratizes it, sharing its blame among ordinary actors rather than declaring it the province of deviants and despots – of Them but not Us. The primary lesson of the Stanford Prison Experiment is that situations can lead us to behave in ways we would not, could not, predict possible in advance.'
>
> Phil Zimbardo

others for no good reason at all, even to think up extra ways to dominate and hurt them, simply because a position of power enables it.

No one knows it's you

One of Zimbardo's conclusions was that the depersonalizing of individuals and the hiding of their identity made the descent into pathological compliance or despicable cruelty easier and more likely: 'When people feel anonymous in a situation, as if no one is aware of their true identity (and thus that no one probably cares), they can more easily be induced to behave in antisocial ways.'

The kind of abusive trolling we see online in social media, where people can hide behind an anonymous user name and don't have to confront the victims they are abusing is a result of the same effect.

Deindividuation

The loss of self-awareness that comes about when people act in groups is known as 'deindividuation'. With their mirrored glasses and uniforms masking their personal identities, the guards are protected by their deindividuation. Conversely, the prisoners are made vulnerable by theirs: stripped or uniformed, with heads shaved or hidden, they are no longer human individuals with whom the guards can empathize. People are easily persuaded they are different, worthless, not deserving of decent treatment. If this can happen among American college students over a period of 36 hours, how much more likely is it to happen in a war, or other stressful situation?

Zimbardo has said that in these situations, past and present disappear and only the gratification of the moment counts. People do things without considering the consequences or the reasons. And no one can say that he or she would not do it. That is why it's so frightening.

CHAPTER 23

What are you waiting for?

Is there something else you should be doing right now, instead of reading this book?

Procrastination: we all do it. There is a task to do, but we just can't or won't settle to it. It doesn't even need to be a boring or unpleasant task – it can still seem nearly impossible to stop wasting time and simply get on with the work or chore that is so important or urgent. Why do we persistently make life difficult for ourselves by putting things off?

Sometimes we procrastinate until there is barely enough time left to complete the task, and then we work better under the pressure we have created. Sometimes we genuinely need to rest for our brains to work subconsciously on a problem.

Is it about doing it right?

It's a common misconception that procrastination is a product of perfectionism – that we put off starting something because we fear we won't do it well enough. In effect, this means we are delaying or avoiding disappointment or frustration by sabotaging the task. It's easier, in terms of one's self-image, to feel that you *could* have done well if you'd tried, than to accept

DISPLACEMENT ACTIVITY

Doing something else instead of the thing you intend or ought to do is called 'displacement activity'. Animals, as well as humans, engage in displacement activity when they can't choose between two actions, or when an action they are strongly motivated to perform is blocked. Some birds will peck at the grass when confronted with an opponent: they can't decide whether to fight or flee, and instead do something entirely useless in the situation.

We sometimes scratch our heads when trying to make a decision – that's a displacement activity. Some people chew or twirl a lock of hair or fiddle with their pen when under pressure or when wrestling with a decision or problem. These are all displacement activities.

that you tried your best and just weren't up to scratch. Of course, sabotaging the task also means sabotaging any possibility of succeeding at it. But studies suggest that there is in fact *no* link with perfectionism and, if anything, perfectionists procrastinate less than non-perfectionists.

Instead, procrastination correlates strongly with conscientiousness – and, curiously, with being a night owl rather than a lark. Procrastinators have less focus on the future, and have a more fatalistic and hopeless view even of the present. It seems as though there is just no point in getting on and doing things because it's not going to work out well anyway.

> **'[Procrastination is] to voluntarily delay an intended course of action despite expecting to be worse off for the delay.'**
>
> Piers Steel, University of Calgary

Feel-good factor

All this sounds rather pessimistic. But procrastination gives us some benefit to offset the longer-term loss. It gives us an immediate boost – we feel good because we are not doing a task we weren't looking forward to doing.

Most of us, with a less-than-optimal dose of willpower, prefer instant gratification over delayed gratification, even if the instant gratification is of a lesser order. It's the 'bird-in-the-hand-worth-two-in-the-bush principle'.

If you ought to wash the car, write a report or put the shopping away, it's easy to defer the task in favour of watching TV or surfing online. You will probably promise yourself that you'll do the dreary task in an hour, or tomorrow. So you feel better immediately because you are doing something you'd rather do, and you also feel better because you have planned to get the task done. You can imagine a future in which the task is done, because it will be done after the time you have set for it. But we are very bad at what psychologists call 'affective forecasting' – imagining how we will feel at some point in the future. So if you plan to write your report tomorrow, you feel happier because you don't have to do it now, and you anticipate that you will feel similarly happy about the plan tomorrow, when you actually have to do the task. Sadly, you won't.

> ### EARLY TO BED . . .
>
> *'Early to bed and early to rise,*
> *Makes a man healthy, wealthy and wise.'*
> This old adage is borne out by research which shows that people who go to bed early and get up early (larks) are less prone to procrastination. As a result they get more done, so they might well be wealthier and are certainly wiser in terms of how they use their time. They probably have better mental health, too, as procrastinators experience a higher level of stress and anxiety overall than non-procrastinators.

Just for kicks

Some people routinely leave tasks until they can only just complete them in time. Do they get a kick out of the adrenaline rush that comes with the stress of struggling to meet an imminent deadline? Dr Joseph Ferrari of DePaul University, Chicago, Illinois, found that procrastinators had two tendencies: either they were delaying a task because they didn't want to do it (avoidance behaviour), or they were delaying it because they believed they worked better under pressure and were waiting until the point at which the task really had to be started if it was to be completed at all. He concluded that this second group was seeking the thrill of the stress they put themselves under. But later studies have suggested this is not the real *reason* for procrastination – it's just the rationalization for it.

THE OPPOSITE OF PROCRASTINATION

Procrastinators can't get going on a task, and when they do tackle it they are often disengaged and do it half-heartedly. The opposite is to experience 'flow' or to be 'in the zone'. 'Flow', as defined by Hungarian-born psychologist Mihaly Csikszentmihalyi, 'is being completely involved in an activity for its own sake. The ego falls away. Time flies. Every action, movement and thought follows inevitably from the previous one, like playing jazz. Your whole being is involved, and you're using your skills to the utmost.'

Studies by Kyle Simpson at Carleton University, Ottawa, Canada, found no correlation between thrill-seekers and procrastination measures. Instead it seems people believe, or tell themselves, that they procrastinate because they work better under pressure or enjoy the rush, but in fact this is just a way of excusing their lack of action to themselves. When doing a task at the last minute, few people are glad they left it so late to start. Many regret the delay, saying they could have done a better job given more time, or that they were interested in the task and it's a shame they didn't have time to enjoy it properly.

A tendency to procrastinate has been linked with damage to or low activation of the prefrontal cortex. This area of the brain plays an important part in planning, impulse control and filtering out distracting stimuli from other parts of the brain.

Most of us don't have a damaged or underactive prefrontal cortex, so we can't use that excuse. Many of us are 'short-termists' who will delay a challenging, dull or long task to do something immediately rewarding – even if it is of little or no long-term value. Most of us procrastinate because we are lazy, lack willpower and are unmotivated. It's just hard to admit – and if we admitted it, we might feel that we actually had to tackle it. And we really can't be bothered.

CHAPTER 24

Who cares if you're outbid on eBay?

Our brains use tricks to make us want what we get, even if we don't get what we want.

Imagine: You are watching a major international sporting event, rooting for your national team. Then a player on the opposing team performs a truly brilliant move. You applaud. Wait – you want him to lose. But how can you want him to lose when he's so good? You have always mocked food-snobs who frequent ridiculously overpriced restaurants. Then someone offers to take you out for a meal at the nearest Michelin-starred establishment. It's against your principles, but you'd love to go, just to try it, just the once. . . . If you've have had an experience like this, you've known cognitive dissonance, described by Leon Festinger in the 1950s.

Does your concern for the environment conflict with your desire for a fuel-hungry car? Would you decide not to buy the car, or buy it and salve your conscience another way?

The 'boring task' experiment

In 1959, Leon Festinger and James Carlsmith carried out an experiment into how people struggle to reconcile a conflict between their actions and their beliefs. They recruited some students to carry out a task, telling them it was part of a psychology experiment into 'measures of performance'. The students were told that two groups of people were doing the experiment and one group had been briefed in advance to give them specific expectations of the task. But this was not true – the real experiment would occur after the task.

The tasks were dull. For half an hour, the students had to move some spools around in a box. Then they had to spend half an hour moving wooden pegs around a board. At the end, the experimenter thanked each student, and said that many people had found the tasks interesting.

> 'If a person is induced to do or say something which is contrary to his private opinion, there will be a tendency for him to change his opinion so as to bring it into correspondence with what he has done or said.'
>
> Leon Festinger and James M. Carlsmith, Stanford University, California

Affecting embarrassment and confusion, the experimenter then told the students that the person briefing the next batch of students hadn't turned up, and asked if they would brief the new group themselves. All they had to do was tell them that the task was really quite interesting. Some students were paid $1 to do this; others were paid $20. Afterwards, the experimenter again said that many people had found the task interesting and they hoped the students had enjoyed it.

Was it really that boring?

There followed an interview about the experiment. One of the questions the interviewer asked was how enjoyable the task was. Remember, the task was really, really boring – but both the experimenter and the students themselves had said it was fun. What was really interesting, though, was that the students who were paid only $1 to lie about the task rated it as more interesting than those who were paid $20.

Festinger and Carlsmith explained this result in terms of cognitive dissonance. The students who had been paid $20 felt they had been adequately rewarded for lying. But the students who had only been paid $1 either had to admit to themselves that they had lied for a small reward, or they had to change their evaluation of the task. It was preferable to admit they had been wrong in their opinion of the task – it wasn't *that* boring, after all.

> '*Humans are not a rational animal, but a rationalizing one.*'
>
> Leon Festinger

Essentially they needed a way to salvage their dignity, and they chose to revise their original experience.

Join the club

It's well known that the harder it is to get into a club, the more membership is prized. Even though the club might be pretty mediocre, with no better facilities than many other clubs, we tell ourselves our effort has been justified because the club is fantastic. In 1956, Elliot Aronson and Judson Mills required people to perform either a humiliating task or a mildly embarrassing task to join a discussion group about sex. The group turned out to be very dull (a discussion about sexual behaviour in animals), but those members who had undergone

Groucho Marx reportedly sent a telegram to the Friar's Club, Beverly Hills, which read: 'PLEASE ACCEPT MY RESIGNATION. I DON'T WANT TO BELONG TO ANY CLUB THAT WILL ACCEPT PEOPLE LIKE ME AS A MEMBER.' The joke is about cognitive dissonance. Groucho wants to join an exclusive club, but has low self-esteem. If the club will accept his membership, it can't be as exclusive as he thought it was, so he doesn't want to join.

the more strenuous initiation enjoyed it anyway. They needed to persuade themselves that their effort had been worthwhile.

Just drink the beer and eat the doughnuts

Few of us have to lie about the boringness of a task (unless perhaps we spend our lives conducting recruitment interviews), but there are plenty of opportunities for cognitive dissonance in everyday life. We might decide to lose weight or eat healthily, but still buy doughnuts in the supermarket. We might resolve not to drink so much, and then buy another bottle of wine. This is dissonance between beliefs and behaviours. We might also exhibit dissonant behaviours – buying a rowing machine on the same shopping trip as buying the doughnuts, for example.

Fun toys and rubbish toys

Apparently, it's not just adults who need to rationalize their behaviour to themselves. Carlsmith was involved in another study, this time in 1963 with Elliot Aronson, investigating cognitive dissonance in young children. In each experiment, a child was left in a room with lots of toys, one of which was extra special. The child was told they could play with any of the other toys, but they would be punished if they played with the special one. Half of the children were threatened with a serious punishment, and half with a mild punishment. None of the children played with the special toy.

Next, all prohibitions were lifted all the children were allowed to play with any toy. Those who had been threatened with a mild punishment were much less likely to play with the special toy than the other children. Carlsmith and Aronson concluded that the children had to rationalize their self-policing response to the mild threat, and did so by persuading themselves that the toy wasn't especially interesting anyway.

In another study, in 2012, four-year-old children were put in the same situation, but some of them were played classical music during the play sessions. Those who heard the music did not devalue the special toy. It seems that music, and some other external stimuli, prevents strategies that reduce dissonance.

'Well, I didn't want it anyway . . . '

Cognitive dissonance is behind a lot of our seemingly petty behaviour. Say, for example, you are outbid for an item in an online auction. You rationalize the situation, feeling relieved you didn't have to spend the money or convincing yourself you didn't really want it that much. It's the same process at work: to remove the dissonant thoughts of disappointment, we immediately devalue the thing that has been lost.

Aesop's famous fable about the fox and the grapes is a perfect example of cognitive dissonance – 'the grapes were sour anyway', says the fox.

When we have to choose between two items or actions, even if the choice seems difficult, we often feel more confident with the choice as soon as it's made. The mind reinforces the choice, to avoid dissonance.

It's not just humans that do this kind of rationalization. In a study in 2007, which used pre-school children and capuchin monkeys, both groups of subjects behaved in the same way. Offered a choice between two items, then a new choice which involved the rejected item and a new item of identical appeal, both children and monkeys chose the new item. There was clearly something wrong with the rejected item, because they'd rejected it. Why would they want it the second time round?

Catastrophe – the world didn't end!

Those of us who don't belong to religious sects built around the belief that the end is nigh quite enjoy mocking the prophesies of doom which pop up every now and then. Festinger (again) and some colleagues decided to study the effects on cult members when these predicted doomsdays came and went without Armageddon occurring. They studied a group called the Seekers who had believed the world would be destroyed by a great flood on the morning of 21 December 1954. Needless to say, it wasn't. The group was led by one Marian Keech (actually Dorothy Martin) who claimed to receive messages from a planet called Clarion; they had expected to be whisked away in an alien spaceship before the flood.

Members had shown considerable commitment, moving from their homes, selling their possessions and leaving their jobs and partners. The day before their anticipated departure, they divested themselves of metal objects, and waited for an alien visitor who was supposed to arrive at midnight and lead them to the spaceship. Midnight came and went, with no alien visitor. How did they react to this disappointment?

It's all good . . .

At 4am, as they all sat in stunned silence, Keech received a message from the aliens saying that God had decided to spare the Earth – that their little group had averted the disaster. The next day, the previously publicity-shy group called the press to tell how they had prevented the catastrophic flood. Unimpressed, the authorities in Chicago threatened Keech with arrest and committal to a mental institution.

As Festinger predicted, the failure of the world to end did not destroy the cult but made it stronger in its proselytizing activity. Instead of realizing that their prophesy had been wrong, the members adjusted what had happened to fit their beliefs – the world *had been* going to end, but their own personal goodness had averted the disaster. The cult had done such a powerful thing that its members could be even more confident in their commitment to it, and they continued to recruit new members. Cognitive dissonance wins the day!

CHAPTER 25

Will smiling make you happy?

Smiling makes us all feel better.
Is this statement true?

People say that if you smile, you'll feel better. It sounds stupid: we smile when we are happy; we aren't happy because we smile. Whatever is wrong in your life won't be fixed by you smiling. But is it really stupid or is there some kernel of truth in this? Psychologists think that there might be.

How do you know what you're like?

We decide what other people are like by watching what they do and listening to what they say. If we see someone pause to give money to a beggar in the street, stop to speak to an elderly neighbour or pick up something a stranger has dropped, we assume they are kind, thoughtful or generous. These are the actions of a kind person, an empathic person, a generous person. On the other hand, if we see someone barge through a crowd, swear at a noisy child or get impatient when an elderly person holds them up by moving slowly, we form a negative opinion of them.

> '*Sometimes your joy is the source of your smile, but sometimes your smile can be the source of your joy.*'
>
> Thich Nhat Hanh, Zen master

If we form a view of other people by their behaviour, perhaps we might form a view of ourselves in the same way. This is called self-perception – the idea that our view of who we are is informed by what we do. We observe ourselves and come to conclusions about our own character, mood and attitudes on the basis of what we see. It sounds ridiculous: surely the way we act manifests how we are, not the other way round?

In 1972 social psychologist Daryl J. Bem, of Cornell University, New York, proposed this theory of self-perception as an alternative to the theory of cognitive dissonance. It has its critics, but at the moment it looks as though both theories have a lot to commend them, affecting people at different times. Self-perception might help people form their view of themselves;

then cognitive dissonance arises if they have to act in a way that contradicts the view they have formed. Self-perception seems to be able to sway our view of ourselves when we haven't already invested a lot in a particular attitude.

'I'm a person who does this'

If we watch what we do and then assume we are the kind of person who does that sort of thing, it should in theory be easy to change attributes we don't like about ourselves. But self-perception can make it more difficult, because we tend to believe that behaviours are more ingrained than they are – they are not just behaviours, but character traits.

If you spent a week lazing on the sofa watching TV and playing video games, you might think, 'I am a lazy person.' If you didn't like that view of yourself, you might then think, 'I have to change and stop being lazy.' That's quite a challenge – it's an open-ended change to your character. It would be more helpful to think, 'I spent a week lazing on the sofa. I don't want to act in a lazy way next week.' A target that relates to a week's activities is much less daunting than a target that seems to require you to rewrite your personality.

ACT DIFFERENTLY TO BE DIFFERENT

French existential philosopher Jean-Paul Sartre believed we make choices about how we are and what we are all the time. A person is defined by what they do, and by that alone. If someone acts in a cowardly way, that makes them a coward. If they stop acting in that way and act bravely, they are no longer a coward but a brave person. We might have an inclination to act one way or another, built up either through past experiences or genetics, but nothing compels us to act or carry on acting like that. It's both a liberating philosophy and a burdensome one – because it states that there is no one else to blame for how you are.

Changing your mind?

Several studies have shown that if students are made to write an essay proposing or defending a view that is the opposite of their own, they tend to adjust their views to come more into line with the argument they have made.

In 1970, Daryl Bem and his colleague Keith McConnell investigated students' views about having control of their own curriculum. The students then had to write an essay proposing the view opposite to their own.

Afterwards, Bem and McConnell asked the students what their views had been at the start of the study. The results did not match their pre-study responses: they had adjusted their views, but claimed that they had always held those views.

For advertisers and others in the business of persuading us, that's good news. They only need to home in on something we haven't really thought about or don't have strong views on, get us to think, say or do something in favour of the view they want us to hold, and we'll believe we were always sympathetic to that view.

Back to boring

Daryl Bem adapted Festinger's experiment – when he made people carry out a boring task (see Chapter 24). Bem's participants listened to a tape recording of a man speaking enthusiastically about the boring task.

One group was told that the man had been paid $20 for his testimonial and the other group was told he had been paid $1. The participants, when questioned, thought the man who had been paid $1 enjoyed the task more than the man who had been paid $20. This is the same result that Festinger got from his participants – those who had been paid only $1 recalled the task as more interesting than those who had been paid $20. Bem concluded that Festinger's subjects were responding in the same way as his own, but the difference was that they were inferring things from their own behaviour rather than from the behaviour of someone else. The process, he argued, was the same – we look at behaviour and infer things about attitude, whether the subject is another person or ourselves.

THE SCIENTIFIC SMILE

The officially accepted smile is called the Duchenne smile. It involves the zygomatic muscles to raise the sides of the mouth and the orbicularis oculi muscles to narrow the eyes. This type of smile is rated by observers as the most genuine.

And earlier . . .

In the 19th century, long before Bem's experiment, William James and Carl Lange came up with a theory now known, unimaginatively, as the James–Lange theory. They proposed that every stimulus – something we feel, notice or experience – has a physiological effect on the body. The physiological

TRICK OR TREAT?

A study carried out in 1979 suggests that if we can see ourselves, we are more likely to act in a way of which we approve. Hidden researchers watched while children went 'trick-or-treating' round their neighbourhood at Halloween. When the occupier of the house left the children alone in the entrance hall, telling them they could choose one sweet from a selection, 33 per cent of the children took more than one sweet. But if there was a mirror in the hallway, so that the children could see what they were doing, less than 4 per cent of them took more than one sweet. It appears that the children didn't want to be seen doing something dishonest, even by themselves, as then they would have to *think of themselves* as dishonest.

effect is processed by the brain and creates an emotion. The physiological response is a reflex.

So if you see a bear running towards you, your hands might start to sweat and your heart begin to race. Then your brain notices the reflex and comes up with fear, and the fear makes you take evasive action. The fear then informs your decision about action.

So – can smiling make you happy?

The difficulty with researching whether smiling makes people happier is that it's necessary to separate the physical act of smiling from a stimulus that might make people happier. It's no use getting people to smile by telling a joke, complimenting

Is she smiling, or not? Difficult to read, the Mona Lisa's expression gives Leonardo's painting an unsettling quality.

them or giving them an ice cream, as all of these might make them happier anyway.

In 1988, a research team headed by Fritz Strack used an ingenious method to get participants to smile. The researchers said they were developing new methods to enable paralyzed people to communicate and needed help working with different ways of holding a pencil using just the muscles of the face.

Some participants had to hold the pencil with their teeth; others had to hold it in their lips. The first method forced the participants' faces into a smile, while the second forced them to adopt an unhappier expression. The participants were then shown cartoons and asked to rate them for humour. The 'smiling' participants found the cartoons funnier.

Real or fake?

A modified version of the study, carried out in 2002, found fake smiling (without raised cheeks) had less of an effect than 'real' smiling (with raised cheeks), and that smiling had an impact on how people perceived positive stimuli but not on their reception of negative stimuli (upsetting or disgusting images). 'Real' smiling still has the effect of lifting mood even if it is faked – it's using all the necessary muscles to replicate a real smile that matters.

So it seems that smiling can, in fact, make you happier. It might be a simple self-perception issue: I'm smiling, so I must be happy. But some physiologists have suggested that as smiling exercises the zygomatic muscles, this changes the blood flow to the brain and might actually produce a real effect on brain chemistry.

DOES IT REALLY TAKE MORE MUSCLES TO FROWN THAN TO SMILE?

It's hard to say exactly how many muscles are used for smiling and frowning, especially as people all smile and frown differently. The simplest recognizable smile uses five pairs of muscles, and the simplest frown uses three muscle pairs. If you are just going for economy of muscle use, frowning is the safer bet. But smiling is better exercise, so perhaps work it into your exercise regime?

CHAPTER 26

Is it really just a stage?

Do children's minds develop through distinct stages, or is their development cumulative and layered?

Your toddler is having tantrums, your eight-year-old is answering back and your teenager is having a strop because you are 'ruining her life'. Don't worry, it's just a stage. They'll grow out of it – everyone says so. But is this true?

Two models for growing out of babyhood

We tend to think of childhood in stages. For parents, the stages can be a bit woolly; sometimes they are very short and specific (the bed-wetting stage, the clingy stage) and at other times they are seemingly interminable (the stroppy teenager stage). This model of 'stages' of childhood makes the child into something like a train that passes through one station after another, picking up and putting down passengers. Oh look, temper tantrums have got on board – they'll be here for a few stops and then they'll get off. But there is a different model that suggests a more gradual development, during which new skills and abilities are piled on top of old ones, accreting eventually into an adult way of engaging with the world. Ways of being are not left behind, but more are added to existing ones.

It's a stage they're going through

The stages model is based on the work of Swiss developmental psychologist Jean Piaget (1896–1980). He divided the learning of young children into four stages, according to the types of skill they acquired and the ways they could interpret and interact with the world:

> **Ages 0–2:** the sensorimotor stage – babies are only aware of their immediate surroundings and themselves. They are highly egocentric and have no idea that something still exists when they can no longer see it (the understanding that objects continue to exist even when they cannot be seen is known as 'object

permanence'). However, studies carried out in 1972 suggest that this theory is inaccurate. If a baby is reaching for an offered object and the lights are turned off, the baby continues to reach for it (as revealed by an infra-red camera).

During the first year of life, small children learn that things are still there even if they can't see them. This newly developed skill of object permanence makes 'peek-a-boo' a fun and reassuring game.

Ages 2–7: the pre-operational stage – children are still centred on the external world and how it works, but can't make logical deductions (which need 'operational' thought). They tend to focus on one aspect of an object or situation at a time. They have difficulty imagining another person's point of view ('theory of mind'), they don't understand principles such as conservation – that the same number of objects can be differently arranged – or the relationship between groups and subgroups of objects. Again, later research suggests that Piaget underestimated what children can do, partly because his experiments were not well designed.

Ages 7–11: the concrete operational stage – children can now understand concepts such as conservation of number and volume, but only with the help of physical (concrete) objects to demonstrate them. Later research once more suggests that Piaget did not frame his experiments in ways that were accessible to children, so again underestimated their abilities.

Ages 11+: the formal operational stage – young people can deal with concepts in their heads and no longer need physical demonstrations to make them real. They can carry out deductive reasoning, understanding, for instance, that if A>B and B>C, then A>C must be true.

Some researchers have found Piaget's tests to be too culturally specific. Pulawat navigators in Polynesia can carry out complex operational thought to navigate their canoes, yet they fail Piaget's tests of development because the tests are meaningless to them.

There has been disagreement, too, about how commonly the fourth stage is ever properly achieved – some research suggests that only a third of the adult population fully achieves the formal operational stage.

Building blocks of behaviour

Jerome Bruner took a different approach, choosing modes rather than stages in development. In 1966, he proposed that three modes of representation overlay each other, building up a set of skills that are not superseded but all still used in adulthood.

Bruner argued that children build a mental 'scaffolding' which supports their learning, with older knowledge supporting new knowledge.

> **Ages 0–1:** the enactive mode – babies use action to interact with the world, building 'muscle memory' (such as learning how to wave and walk – skills that are not forgotten except in cases of brain injury).

> **Ages 1–6:** the iconic mode – reality is represented through images and sounds.

Ages 7+ the symbolic mode – information is stored and manipulated using symbols such as language and mathematics.

Bruner discovered that if an adult first talked some of Piaget's tasks through with the child, they would be less likely to fail. So, if the child was asked, before pouring water from a tall, thin glass into a short, wide glass, whether there would be more, less or the same amount of water after he had poured it, he was more likely to give the right answer. Combining all modes (enactive, iconic and symbolic) made it easier to understand what was happening. If children used a ball of plasticine to make different shapes while simultaneously explaining what they were doing, they readily understood the conservation of volume – even if they had failed Piaget's conservation tests.

THINKING THE UNTHINKABLE?

A person's schemas can be structured so that a useful relationship between them is impossible. For example, someone's schema for 'marriage' and their schema for 'homosexuality' might make the concept of gay marriage incomprehensible to them – they can't see how the two words can go together and mean anything. If that person is not willing or able to adjust their schemas so that a fit is possible, they will have to reject gay marriage. Interestingly, people who do reject ideas like this often use words like 'unthinkable' or 'inconceivable' – and that's exactly what such concepts are to them.

Inside out or outside in?

Piaget's model is based on development happening from within the child, in a set sequence. Although development requires interaction with the environment and other people, the child is the key component and instigator.

Bruner took a different view, making the environment and other people much more important – children's learning is enabled by adults and other children. It is through their interaction with others that children come to impart meaning to their actions and sounds. If a child reaches for something and can't grasp it, an adult passes the object to them. They then learn that reaching for something acts as pointing, as that's how it is interpreted. Pointing then becomes an action with its own meaning – a meaning bestowed by the actions of others. This is an 'outside in' way of learning, with influence from the outside world helping to build the child's cognition.

FERAL CHILDREN AND MISSED CHANCES

Every so often children are discovered living solely with wild animals, having been kept isolated from human contact. These tragic cases provide rich pickings for psychologists who can then track the children's development when exposed to other humans, language, and normal human activities and environments.

Children brought up by wolves or wild dogs often run on all fours, howl and growl, and eat raw meat – in other words, they act in the same ways as their canine siblings. If found early enough they can sometimes integrate into human society. They can learn a language, start to eat cooked food and walk upright. Others who have missed human contact for longer might never acquire language or integrate into human society. There seems to be a cut-off point somewhere between the ages of six and 13. If a child fails to learn a language before that, they might never be capable of language learning.

How to build a working brain

To make their brains fit for normal, independent life, children have a lot of work to do. First, they build the schemas that they need in order to structure knowledge (see Chapter 20). Then they assimilate new knowledge by fitting it into their schemas, and they modify their schemas to accommodate information that won't fit into them. Luckily, children don't need to know that they are doing it.

In fact, we carry on doing this throughout our lives, some of us more willingly than others. When you meet someone with very entrenched views who simply rejects as 'nonsense' anything they don't want to think about, you are seeing someone who has given up schema-building. There is no place in their schema-set for internet banking or modern art and they can't begin to think about it. It's not the same as investigating it and saying 'no thank you' – it's having a 'closed mind', one in which the schemas have fossilized. The tendency is marked in older people, but we sometimes encounter young people who seem unwilling or unable to take new ideas on board.

Keeping an open mind about new ideas indicates that we are still schema-building.

As children grow older, they become capable of 'operations' – higher order mental structures that require logical relationships between schemas. Operations make more complex understanding possible. Again, we can see operational failures in people who are resistant to new ideas.

Blank slate or formatted hard drive?

There is an age-old concept of the baby's mind as a *tabula rasa* – a blank slate waiting for knowledge to be written on it. But there are many challenges to this view. Instinctive and reflex actions are hardwired into the brain; the infant has an instinct to suckle and does this within minutes of being born, if given the opportunity. There might be innate schemas, ready to be populated with knowledge – so instead of a blank slate, a baby's brain is more like a formatted hard drive with the structures ready to hold knowledge already in place.

Noam Chomsky has made a case for language falling into this category, with the child born ready 'primed' to learn language. Chomsky has pointed to the syntactical similarities between languages that make it possible for a baby to populate its schema with whichever language is used by the family.

CHAPTER 27

Is it worth doing the lottery?

Do you buy lottery tickets?
Oddly, it might be better if
your numbers don't come up.

Do you dream of winning the lottery, or of some other stroke of fortune that will make you instantly rich? Many of us have listed the things we'd buy and do if we suddenly had immense wealth. And there are plenty of businesses and national lotteries that feed off those dreams. But would it really make you happy?

A tax on stupidity?

Why do you buy a lottery ticket, or place a bet at the bookmaker's? Do you really think you might win? Do you hope you might win, even though you know you probably won't? Or is it just 'a bit of fun'? What exactly is the fun in handing over money in exchange for a vanishingly small chance of winning so much money it will probably make you miserable?

In 1961, Viv Nicholson won the then-huge sum of £152,319 on the UK football pools. She soon spent her money and ended up in debt and in trouble with the law. One of her five husbands died when he crashed the car she had bought him with her winnings. Her photo is featured on the cover of The Smiths' 'Heaven Knows I'm Miserable Now'.

It's well known that many people who gamble can ill afford it. There's an arrogant assumption among the better off that these people are stupid – they are wasting money they can't afford on the virtually non-existent chance of winning. But they're not. They're buying something certain and positive – the opportunity to dream of a better life. Buying the ticket is a passport out of the struggle of everyday life, but it's a tourist visa, not an emigration permit. For the days or hours between buying the ticket and hearing the disappointing result, the ticket-holder is permitted to dream of a better life. It's no more a waste of money than any other transient pleasure, such as a glass of wine or a good meal. The point of the ticket is not winning – it's dreaming of winning.

Be careful what you wish for . . .

Most lottery winners mess up. Studies have found that between 70 per cent and 90 per cent of US lottery winners are broke again within five years – and that's not the worst of it. Apart from poverty, their spending on drugs, drink, prostitutes, extravagant consumer goods and dodgy business deals has led many winners to physical and mental ill-health, crime, suicide and even violent death. Several have killed others or themselves in drug- or drink-fuelled accidents.

Most people unused to wealth need help dealing with it – otherwise they end up like those overpaid teen stars who go off the rails. The winners who do best in terms of managing their lives are often those who use the money for good causes – giving to charity or setting up a trust fund.

So why can't we deal with getting what we think we want?

It's all relative

A study carried out in the USA in 1978 by Philip Brickman and Dan Coates measured the happiness levels of lottery winners and of paralyzed accident victims – two sets of people who had experienced significant changes in fortune. It also studied a control group of people unaffected by either an accident or a win. They found that two processes, contrast and habituation, led to lottery winners being less happy than we might expect.

Peaks and troughs

The point at which a person learns of their lottery win is generally one of ecstatic excitement – it is usually a 'peak experience'. It is very difficult for later events to match up to the glory of that moment, so the delight people take in smaller pleasures tends to diminish. Lottery winners have been found to enjoy day-to-day pleasures less than people who have not won the lottery.

This doesn't just apply to winning the lottery. Anyone in a career that reaches a height and then fades away – especially one that peaks in youth – has to deal with this issue. What does a prime minister do after losing office? Why do ex-sports stars and ex-supermodels sometimes find themselves on a personal downward spiral? Achieving a peak ambition can lead to a sense of emptiness and lack of direction in its aftermath.

> '**You aren't buying a chance to win, because there is really no probability that you will win. You are buying the right to fantasize about winning.**'
>
> Derek Thompson, business editor at *The Atlantic* magazine

Striving for something gives our lives purpose, one that disappears if we achieve our goal. Astrophysicist Dame Jocelyn Bell Burnell, who was controversially excluded from the Nobel prize for physics for her discovery of pulsars (the Nobel prize committee gave the credit to her thesis supervisor, Antony Hewish) has said that she is glad she didn't win, as where would there be left to go? She wouldn't be able to take as much pleasure in other prizes as they'd never match up to the Nobel. She has since been showered with honours, including a damehood.

Jocelyn Bell Burnell makes the most of not having won a Nobel prize for her discovery of pulsars.

Winner's (bad) luck

Even the pleasures we imagine we we'd enjoy if we were rich diminish over time as we become accustomed to them. Habituation makes them less special. People quickly become used to their home always being warm, to always having the best food and going to the best hotels and restaurants. Apparently, people can even become jaded by being driven by a chauffeur in a flashy car and sipping cocktails on palm-fringed beaches. The exotic becomes mundane.

At the same time, it becomes harder to take pleasure in small events such as receiving a compliment or watching a favourite television programme. The lottery winners reported less enjoyment of these things than either the control group or the accident victims. Nor did they expect to be happier in the future. Over the long term, the winners had no gain in happiness over the control group.

When Brickman and Coates questioned victims of serious accidents, whose fortunes had therefore taken a major downturn, the researchers discovered that they, too, contrasted their previous life with their current situations. The comparison made them more miserable, especially as they tended to

LUCKY NUMBERS?

Some people always buy the same lottery numbers, often choosing ones that have some personal significance, such as a string of birthdates or a number they consider 'lucky'. The more times their numbers don't come up, the better they think their chances are of winning in the near future. Even if they know the maths, they engage in some kind of mystical thinking that encourages them to believe that every number must have its turn. In fact, there is no greater likelihood that a random sequence of numbers will appear than that a sequence like 1, 2, 3, 4, 5 and 6 will come up.

The website for the UK lottery publishes a list of the numbers that win most and least, and of those most 'overdue' – those that haven't come up for a while. But every draw is random, of course, and the results of previous draws have no impact on future results. It could be that the same six numbers appear every week for a year – it's just not very likely.

But if you *do* want to play the lottery, and do want to risk winning lots of money, don't pick the same numbers that everyone else chooses. This means avoid following an obvious pattern. Of course, if you want to win only a modest amount to limit the damage the win does to your life, picking – say – the first six prime numbers should guarantee that if your numbers do come up you will have to share them with lots of other people.

view their past situation through rose-tinted spectacles, remembering it as more pleasurable than it really seemed at the time. This heightened their sense of loss.

PICTURE CREDITS